The Weak Send Rocks, The Strong Send Rockets

Marek Arnaud

Eloquent Books
New York, New York

Eloquent Books

An imprint of AEG Publishing Group

845 Third Avenue, 6th Floor - 6016

New York, NY 10022

www.eloquentbooks.com

ISBN 978-1-60860-201-8

Printed in the United States of America

Book Design: Linda W. Rigsbee

To my father

Seven days without laughter makes one weak.

Joel Goodman

Contents

Foreword

BY HON. GOUGH WHITLAM AC QC,

FORMER PRIME MINISTER OF AUSTRALIA (FROM 1972 TO 1975)

For more than four centuries French statesmen and diplomatists have inspired the world with elegant aphorisms. I am flattered to be asked to introduce a collection of aphorisms by the author of this book, who has lived in Sydney from January 2001 to July 2004.

In 1972 France's representatives in Australia were impressed by my response to the announcement by the Prime Minister who preceded me that the elections to the House of Representatives would be held on December 2nd. I pointed out that it was the anniversary of the battle of Austerlitz, where Napoleon I, Emperor of the French, defeated the ramshackle and reactionary coalition of Franz I, Emperor of Austria, and Alexander I, Emperor of Russia. In 1989 the Australian Foreign Minister, Gareth Evans, highlighted my support for an event which occurred in France sixteen years before Austerlitz. He chose me as the President of Honor of the Australian National Council for the Celebration of the Bicentenary of the French Revolution 1989.

During the author of this book's residence in Sydney there has been a remarkable resurgence of interest in French exploration of the Pacific and Indian Oceans. In 2001 the helicopter-carrier *Jeanne-d'Arc* visited Sydney to celebrate the Centenary of the Federation of the Australian colonies. In 2002 at many of Sydney's cultural institutions there were exhibitions to commemorate the bicentennial of the sojourn of Nicolas-Thomas Baudin and Louis-Claude de Saulces de Freycinet in Sydney.

At a time when there has been tension in Australia about the propriety of engaging in overseas wars, it is salutary to recall that by far the largest Australian military commitments and casualties were in France in World War I, when Australia's population was only one quarter as large as it is today.

The people of Sydney have been fortunate to have in the author of this book a French person who was educated in southern France, Iowa (U.S.A.), and Cambridge (U.K.) and who has worked in Leningrad, Madrid, Warsaw, Vienna, Geneva, New York, and Tel Aviv. All these places are relevant in debates taking place in Australia today. His succinct thoughts are soundly based and should be widely quoted.

Gough Whitlam, May 2004

Acknowledgements

Apart from all the anonymous people who were my involuntary sources of inspiration, I wish to acknowledge my native English-speaking proof-readers Professors Ken Dutton (Newcastle University, Australia) and Ross Steele (University of Sydney, Australia), and my main provider of Internet jokes Cyrille van Heyst (who forwarded them from Adjunct Professor Philip A. Neck, Southern Cross University, Australia) as well as my editor, Angela Randolph.

About The Illustrator

Lionel Portier's editorial cartoons and illustrations have appeared in various newspapers around the world. He worked as a regular contributor for *Le Monde* in France, *The South China Morning Post* in Hong Kong and *The Sydney Morning Herald*, *The Australian Financial Review* and *The Age* in Australia. These black and white drawings are extracted from a series of published and unpublished satirical cartoons that originated during Lionel's last year of study at the ENSAVC art school in Brussels in the years 1989-1990, as the world was oscillating from one order to another. During the following decade, Lionel has lived in Sydney, Australia, where he taught graphic arts and worked as a free-lance illustrator and graphic designer. He is now back in Europe, sharing his time between France and Switzerland.

TABLE OF ILLUSTRATIONS

Preface

As the Japanese *haiku* writer, the diplomat is most often encouraged by necessity to concentrate his or her thoughts into very few words. This requirement for clarity and simplicity is enhanced by today's media-driven world: long sentences in fact sentence you to indifference or oblivion.

The present volume is the result of several years of my observation and listening, spanning from 1989 to 2008, in successive multilateral or bilateral jobs in Geneva, New York, Tel Aviv, and Sydney. The following aphorisms or one-liners have been inspired to me by involuntary slips of the tongue, associations of ideas or wordplays. They are meant to show that, even when dealing with serious subjects, some sense of humor allows one to keep things in perspective. If anyone mentioned or alluded to in this book felt offended, this would be unintentional on the part of the author.

As a French international worker trained to use the English language, I have attempted both to take advantage of the amazing flexibility of that international idiom and to express some perceptions that my national culture has perhaps prepared me to feel more acutely than non-French observers. This is said with the utmost humility and modesty, in order to contradict the reputed arrogance that my unfortunate fellow countrymen have been thought to be prone to display.

The various chapters of this book have been arranged according to reverse chronological order, like in resumes, so as to go from the more recent to the more distant memories. The latter ones may include more "private" jokes covering less public subjects and requiring some endnotes, as Chapter 2 may need for a non-Australian public.

The Chapter called "*Addendum*" is a collection of aphorisms, quotes and jokes which have been forwarded to me by friends on the Internet, and whose authors remain anonymous. I do not claim authorship of any of them but wish to pay tribute to their actual authors for their sense of humor.

The last Chapter is devoted to some untranslatable French puns, which may appeal to the French-speakers among the readers.

International Aphorisms

(Geneva, 2004–2008)

1 – INTERNATIONAL BITS AND PEACE

With an African-American president,
will the White House need to be renamed?

A new motto for American leisure-seekers:
"Yes, week-end."

In international relations, some resort to force, others to farce.

The nonproliferation regime is not liked by proliferating
regimes.

Global warming makes people get cold feet.

There is also a political climate change.

Those who try to make some states, failed states
sometimes succeed.

In a financial crisis, the main task for all is: "Save the savings!"

With the international financial crisis, golden parachutes no longer guarantee a soft landing.

Some "freedom fighters" actually fight not for freedom but against it.

A few terrorists have taken a pilot crash course.

Every one has his/her own bin laden with trash.

With regard to terrorism, one should have a ground zero tolerance.

A post-9/11 prayer: "Have mercy on U.S."

The George W. Bush administration had its pros and neocons.

The international community wanted to ban weapons of mass destruction. Then it went after the destruction of the Taliban's weapons.

Terrorism is a third-world phenomenon.
This is a third-World War.

The one good thing about suicide bombers: they cannot be multiple offenders.

With Air Marshals on some flights, if you meet a friend named Jack on a plane, don't say "Hi!" to him.

Some countries are run by butchers.
They make you want to become vegetarian.

Although it was run by the Baath Party,
the Iraqi regime was not clean.

An American war in Iraq without the U.N.
was UN-American.

After eliminating pockets of resistance in Iraq,
the U.S. had to put its hand in its pockets for reconstruction.

Developing countries need experts on exports
and not the export of experts.

In Iraq, American soldiers are fed up with their combat
uniform. This phenomenon is called "fatigue fatigue."

The U.S. has unilateral relations with all the countries of
the world.

Dubbing a president "Dubya" was dubious.

Some guided missiles are sent by misguided leaders.

Some Palestinians would have liked to see Sharon stoned.

A lesson sometimes forgotten: if you send your troops for a trip
they may trip into a trap.

The message from many French voters: "Write off Le Pen."[1]

The French eat snails because they don't like fast food.

A child who had a grandmother in Poland was asked how he
called her. He answered, "On the phone."

Debt

New job prospects in Europe:
mad-cowboy, foot-and-mouth doctor.

Let us be frank:
the euro is a success.

In some countries, women are sentenced to be stoned.
Those countries are still in the Stone Age.

A solution to hunger in the world is food for thought
but has to be palatable.

Baghdad,
Bad guy,
Body bags.

Now that there are casinos in Moscow,
you can play Russian roulette safely.

A change of régime:
some countries used to be run by counts,
now they are run by accountants.

Cultural differences between Europeans and Americans:
we like opera; they prefer Oprah.[2]

Will a wider Europe be a wilder Europe?

An ailing Pope in Rome:
it's the Holy Wait and See.

Baghdad

How is it possible to be upbeat on Downing Street?

A conference was bogged down on procedure:
it argued about paragraph 2 b) or not 2 b).

There should be red lines for the Red Cross not to cross.

One military said, "Those who want to ban mines are not
friends of mine."

What makes some governments irate: IRA, Iran, Iraq.

Those who want to enrich uranium
run the risk of impoverishing their countries.

In negotiating a peace accord, some pursue ideals,
others just deals.

I don't like soccer:
it's is not my World Cup of tea.

Supporter

2 – ASIA

Korea is the soul of Asia.

A President named Megawati could not lack energy.

In Japan, 'r' and 'l' are often confused. That's why they like
general elections.

Bangkok has friendly ties with many people.

Japan preserved its civilization:
it didn't change it one Toyota.

Heard on the radio in Fiji:
"A new government plan on water distribution is in the
pipeline."

Turkey was called "the sick man of Europe."
India is the Sikh man of Asia.

Australia should not be timorous about Timor.

In the United Arab Emirates,
you Dubai tax-free goods.

Muslim countries are conservative:
nothing new under the Sunni.

China is fragile and can break up.

Rapid Growth

3 – MISCELLANEOUS

People are fed up with urban violence:
they want to live in cities not in atrocities.

Morning shower, foggy day, quiet night:
my life looks like a weather report.

Every man has a grey area,
especially after fifty.

Character changes with age:
less boldness, more baldness.

A man reading a sign on a wall:
"Who is this Bill Posters,[3] and what has he done for being
prosecuted?"

A parish priest was found selling church artifacts;
he was a "Thou art" dealer.

Some works of art make dollars
even if they don't make sense.

A CEO to his former counterpart after a hostile takeover:
"Good to have your company."

Instead of handling a lawsuit at the Bar, a lawyer went to a bar
in his suit. He ended up behind bars and that didn't suit him.

Bartenders should accept a Bar Code of Conduct.

A tired tennis player in a sigh:
"Give me a tie break!"

A prostitute became a writer:
she changed her body of work.

An improbable ad: "Porn star seeking new position."

If policemen acted in an erotic film,
viewers would eat pop-corn while watching cop-porn.

Men like to play golf because it requires a lot of balls.

You may be an aspiring leader
but you take aspirin like anyone else.

People give human features to things:
they call toilets 'male', 'female' or 'disabled'.

Have you ever seen a red light camera?
It is neither red nor light.

If you think your anti-wrinkle cream is not efficient,
try to imagine what your face would look like without it.

The blindness of Justice is in the eye of the beholder.

To face the crisis, some airlines will need to tighten the seatbelt.

Economy Class, Business Class, First Class.
Who said the class warfare is over?

An airplane that crashes without any apparent reason should
be called a Dumbo jet.

Those who drink to others' health
often harm their own.

Some writers are better at the four-letter word than at the
foreword of a letter.

An angry patron at a lousy restaurant: "I ordered salmon, not
salmonella!"

More and more often you can see a "non-smoking" sign.
This is a good sign.

As a result of the tobacco ban on the workplace,
where there is smoke there are fired people.

A man in his swimming suit was thrown out of a bar.
He was looking for the pool room.

Some governments should have a Minister for
Extra-Marital Affairs.

A stockbroker's lunch:
fish 'n' bluechips.

When they send their invoices, some surgeons confuse the
operation table with the multiplication table.

What city-dwellers want:
more taxis, less taxes.

A musician had children:
he played Haydn while they played hide and seek,
and he wrote suites while they ate sweets.

Art is becoming a product:
more and more often we can hear chamber of commerce
music.

A board can be bored when, after a minute's silence,
it has to read minutes in silence.

The difference between polite and impolite people:
the former say "Hello", the latter just say "Hell."

Sometimes a memorandum of understanding is hard to
understand.

Will Santa Claus come this year?
He is toying with the idea.

Santa Claus? The name rings a bell.

Banks are like trees:
they have branches that can crush you.

Politicians are like bras:
you choose them for support and they hide the truth.

A womanizer said he preferred women over 50.
But he meant bra size.

The Church condemns cardinal sins,
but often not the Cardinals' sins.

Some fast-food restaurants only provide plastic cutlery.
Are they afraid of being hijacked?

Advice to drivers:
while at the wheel, don't try to reinvent it.

Some cars carry a 'Baby on Board' sign.
Does that mean that cars without it can be hit unreservedly?

You can train in a park but you can't park in a train.

Why do girls who drink Coca-Cola® have the shape of a
Perrier® bottle and vice-versa?

A man stopped his car near a woman hitch-hiking
but realized she needed a facelift more than a lift.

A suspect arrested by the police refused to talk to the media.
He did not want to make any off-the-handcuff comments.

If some people put their money where their mouth is,
they would choke to death.

Who said politicians are not fit?
They run for office, then run the country and finally run away.

The more (husbands), the merrier (widow).

If you are reckless, the sum you pay to drive on the freeway
may be the death toll.

A gay person can be sad too.

A blanket solution may be a cover-up.

A mobile phone smuggled into a prison deserves to be called a
cell phone.

Some members of Congress attend hearings on foreign aid
using a foreign hearing aid.

Most washing machines are racist:
they don't mix white with color.

Very few Hollywood film-makers think out of the box
office.

Corpses would love to think out of the box.

Our ancestors had Martin Luther. Our parents had
Martin Luther King. We are left with Larry King.

A man tried to comfort a door:
he had read a sign saying it was alarmed.

4 – INFORMATION TECHNOLOGY (IT)

A once famous U.S. website: george.www.bush.

Feminists still hesitate to use the Internet:
they are afraid of being accused of accepting e-males.

Music on the Internet? Why not a symphony in e-major?

The new economy:
no more hard work, only hardware and network.

When the racist websites are prohibited, your PC[4] will be PC.[5]

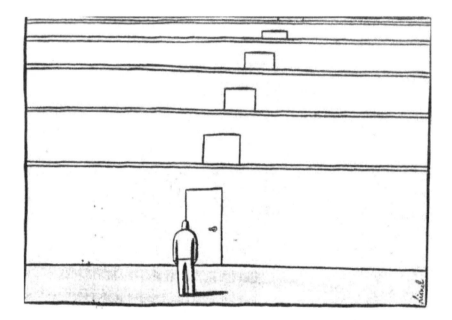

The First Step

Remember when chips were for eating, the net was for catching fish, and the web for catching flies?

A PC is the only place where a copycat is subject to a mouse.

How can plain people become computer literate when they hear, "this PC is Y2K-OK"?[6]

The "net economy" is now in net losses.

A slow printer can be called an ink-jet lag.

An inmate asked for a computer in his cell: he wanted to press the "Escape" key.

European computers use PowerPoint®. American ones use Superpower Point.

5 – DEFINITIONS

A baby boomer is NOT a noisy child.

Frequent flyers are NOT men who unzip their pants often.

A ten-year bond is NOT an old "007" film.

A homogeneous population is NOT necessarily
composed of gay bright scientists.

A Chairman is NOT necessarily
an old man in a wheelchair.

A "short black" is NOT
an indigenous dwarf.[7]

A minimum is NOT
a short mother.

Something transparent does NOT
go through your father and mother.

A drinking vessel is NOT
a naval ship with partying sailors.

A posthumous piece is NOT
a dish you eat after a Lebanese appetizer.[8]

A U2 plane is NOT
a rock group aircraft.

An undercover garage is NOT
a car park for discreet policemen.

Pole dancing is NOT
an Arctic form of entertainment.

The box office is NOT
a place where you get punched.

A diatribe is NOT
a group of people careful about what they eat.

A headquarter is NOT
twenty-five percent of a brain.

A serial killer is NOT
a person who destroys corn flakes.

Zebra is NOT
the name of a female garment said with a French accent.

Recycling does NOT mean
riding a bike twice.

A food court is NOT
a place where products are tried.

An exhibitionist is NOT
a specialist in art display.

Ideology is NOT the study of idiocy.

Mediocrity is NOT necessarily
a characteristic of the media.

Down-Under Aphorisms

(Sydney, 2001-2004)

1 – AUSTRALIA

Even Down Under,
they have ups and downs.

In Sydney Harbor,
you can hear a lot of ferry tales.

Everyone has their amusement park: the U.S. has Disney,
Australia has Sydney.

Some diplomats complain about boredom in Canberra:
for them it's capital punishment.[9]

The Australians made a film about Moulin-Rouge for the
Cannes Festival: it was French Cannes-Cannes for
French Can-Canberra.

The Australian conservative government had two allies:
the bush and Bush.

Australia's exports changed from raw materials to movie stars:
from nickel to Nicole.[10]

Actual graffiti seen on road signs in Sydney:
Form One (P)Lane(T),
and *Red Light (District) Ahead.*

With its Pacific asylum policy, the Australian Government
turned refugees into re-Fijis[11].

Australia used to tell refugees: "Welcome aboard."
Then it told them: "Welcome abroad."

To some Ministers
migrants give migraine.

On the issue of racism in Australia,
the situation is not all black and white.

Qantas® is preoccupied with quantity.
Australia needs another airline called Qalas.

If you think the Australian population is only made of surfers,
you're only looking at the surface.

Some Australian businessmen prefer meeting around a surfboard than around a board table.

A Sydney gay student was very popular in Britain: he was Oxford's treat.[12]

Australia has one Queen.[13]
Sydney has many queens.

Those who want same-sex marriages would like to see the bride side of life.

Considering their fees, some Australian lawyers should be called barristars.

Because of its price, real estate in Sydney should be called surreal estate.

The Australian government's policy to fight the bushfires is under fire.

An Australian judge's advice to the Police:
"Don't Tampa[14] with evidence."

Australia now has a multicultural society: people named Ahmed or Aaron are no longer required to give their Christian names.

Insecurity

In times of crisis,
the voters want security not generosity.

Many Australian voters realized how appalling Hanson[15] was.

If pageant contests took place among politicians,
they could be named Miss Lead, Miss Conduct, Miss
Management, Miss Guided, or Miss Fortune.

In some hospitals the waiting list is so long that a patient
deserves that name.

Hopefully all Tasmanian forests will not be turned into timber.
Touch wood.

The Australian media was charged with attempted Murdoch.[16]

The Middle East Piece–By–Piece Process

(Tel Aviv, 1996-2000)

1 – INTRODUCTION

The following aphorisms have been inspired in the author by his professional life. He worked in Israel from September 1996 to December 2000. Although the subject may sometimes seem serious or even tragic, the sense of humor that is intended here is directly derived from the author's extensive contacts with both local Israeli and Palestinian people, who have demonstrated that they can also take such an attitude to survive the conflict. May it be taken as a sympathetic tribute to their resilience to suffering, and an expression of hope that a just and lasting peace will someday prevail in that region.

2 – WAR AND PEACE IN THE MIDDLE EAST

A) THE PROCESS

Some prefer the process to the peace.

After signing an agreement, the parties have a banquet.
It is called the peace meal.

In the Middle East peace process, you need to be dead serious
about the deadline
in order to break the deadlock.

The peace process is back at Rabin Square[17] one.

The middle of the road to peace
is hard to find in the Middle East.

The peace process has its pros and its icons.

In peace talks, those who use foot-dragging
may shoot themselves in the foot,
especially when an agreement is at hand.

Some Middle East leaders want peace,
dead or alive.

In order to make headway in peace talks and hit the headlines,
you may need to bang heads together.

The peace process players sometimes use trump cards.
Now they can gamble in Jericho.[18]

In the peace process, some offer committees,
others want commitments.

On the implementation of peace accords, some leaders give
instructions,
others practice obstruction.

In the peace process some take a settlement into account,
others only want a settlement of accounts.

For making peace, some leaders think they have a mission,
others that they have permission.

Palestinians are preoccupied with the right of return.
Many Israelis are worried about the return of the Right.

When there are too many mediators in the peace process,
the parties may say, "Leave us in peace!"

When the peace process comes up against a blank wall,
it is often the Wailing Wall.

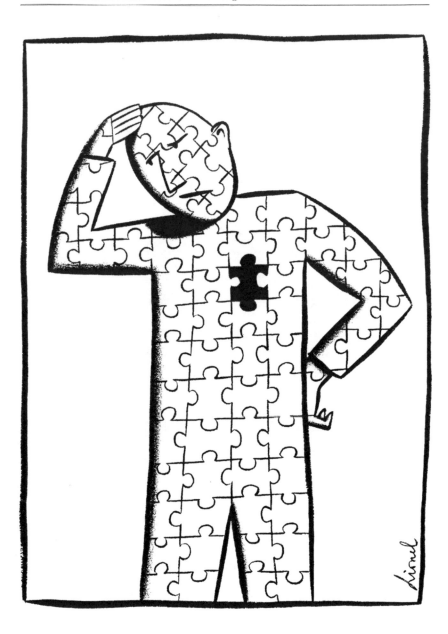

The Missing Piece

After riots, some are tempted to address the Oslo process
by saying, "May it rest in peace!"

In the Middle East, there is only a lot of attention
when there is a lot of tension.

In the 50-year conflict, the chances of peace appear to be 50-50.

A lesson for negotiators: when peace is around the corner,
don't corner your opponent.

The closure of an agreement may end
the closure of the Palestinian Territories.

The closure of the Palestinian Territories
is an open question.

The issue of Jerusalem
is of capital importance.

The unification of Jerusalem is a divisive issue.

In Jerusalem, pressure mounts
on Temple Mount.[19]

The accords provided for withdrawal from the occupied
territories by stages.
Meanwhile, the leaders occupied the stage.

The Oslo Process:
Oh! Slow Process!

Some throw stones at soldiers.
Some former generals[20] throw sand in people's eyes.

An Israeli will never dare a Palestinian to cast the first stone.

Sometimes the Israeli leaders remain stone deaf
to the Palestinian stones.

In the Middle East everyone is within a stone's throw of
someone else.

The road to peace in the Middle East is still rocky.

The weak ones send rocks,
the strong ones send rockets.

Some Israeli officials confuse the final status
with the status quo.

Those who dream of a New Middle East
should keep in mind the Old Middle West.

With all the meetings that were supposed to pave the way to
peace, the Middle East should be covered with roads.

Peace

In the Middle East, some see nations,
others hallucinations.

Gunmen, not guns, should be fired.

When the land is occupied,
the leaders are preoccupied.

Extremists belong to political circles.
Those are vicious circles.

At the table of negotiations, it often takes time
to negotiate a time table.

There still is a gulf between Israel and the Arab countries.

After terrorist acts, messages of sympathy are addressed to
'innocent victims', as if there were guilty ones.

Wasn't the State of Israel founded on a unilateral declaration
of independence? Do unto others. . .[21]

Israel has apparently learned a lot from the Soviet Union motto:
"What is mine is mine, what is yours is negotiable."

Will the Wye Plantation accord[22]
contain the seeds of peace?

Vicious Circle

In the Middle East when the ball is sent into the other's court,
it is often a cannon ball.

Some Arabs claim Israel is not part of the Middle East.
The way Israel sometimes negotiates shows they are wrong.

After the conflict comes cooperation:
after irritation comes irrigation.

A goal for peacemakers: replace terrorism with tourism,
and attacks with a tax.

Peace dividends: after the mine fields,
a gold mine.

A motto for peace education:
"After the clashes, the classes."

Sometimes the fruits of peace
are left to rot.

When a peace deal is concluded,
some say, "Big deal!"

Who says the Arab media doesn't have any freedom of
expression? It is free to criticize Israel without limits.

Israelis and Palestinians have one thing in common:
every morning, they may end up mourning someone.

It is always better to trade barbs in a diplomatic conference
than to deploy barbed wire on the ground.

A package deal is part and parcel of the negotiation.

In the Middle East, words change meaning when lines are
crossed:
liberation for some means occupation for others.

On the "an-eye-for-an-eye" doctrine
Israelis and Arabs see eye to eye with each other.

Sometimes peace is a pipe dream that goes up in smoke.

When they met,
Barak,[23] Mubarak,[24] and Chirac[25] talked about Iraq.

After sticking to one's guns for so long,
it is hard to put them back on the racks.

It is usually when the Israeli generals leave the Army
that they order it to leave occupied lands.

In the Middle East a nuclear reactor
calls for some reaction.

With regard to the final-status talks,
one had to read between Barak's "red lines."

Weaning

Many people ask what the price of peace will be.
They don't ask what the cost of war is.

Roadblocks may be stumbling blocks on the path to peace.

What peace is all about:
less tanks and more think tanks.

First, enemies exchange fire, then prisoners, then signatures,
and finally ambassadors.

A goal for Israeli tourists: have coffee in Amman
to meet Kofi Annan.

In the Middle East no one should
fuel rumors about oil.

There are Israeli Arabs.
Will there be Palestinian Jews?

B) SETTLEMENTS

Israeli settlements in the West Bank can be an obstacle
to a peace settlement in the Middle East.

A freeze of the settlements is not warmly welcome in Israel.
This is a hot issue.

Enemy Brothers

The building of Israeli settlements and the demolition of
Palestinian homes are not confidence-building measures.

Concrete buildings in the Palestinian Territories
do not provide concrete answers.

The Israeli settlers call the peace process a plot against them.
They only want to save their plot of land.

When some Israelis say they need room for building in the
Palestinan Territories, there is no room for optimism.

The Netanyahu[26] Government by-passed peace accords
to build by-pass roads in the Palestinian Territories.

C) SYRIA – LEBANON

Ehud Barak was serious about the Syrians.

Israel replied to Syria's demands that it cannot negotiate by fax.
This is a fax of life.

Many feared that, when Israel withdrew from Lebanon,
Syria would withdraw from the peace process.

When Israel meets Syria,
it will be tea for two around 242.[27]

Israel's withdrawal from Lebanon
is Revolution 425.[28]

The Israeli arguments about the Syrians' access to the Sea of
Galilee are fishy.

Israel and Syria are not on the same 1967 line.

Barak's message to Hezbollah in a nutshell: "Stop shelling."

There are two reasons why Israel doesn't want to leave the
Golan Heights: water and wine.

There are divisions in Israel
about Israeli divisions leaving the Golan.

D) WATER & SEA

On the issue of water in the Middle East
many are thirsty for agreement.

Regarding negotiations on water
there are too many leaks.

For many years negotiators on water
have been treading water.

Differences over the Jordan River can be bridged
if demands are watered down.

Invoking the U.N. Charter with regard to Israel's naval actions
would be sailing uncharted waters.

On Mediterranean cooperation, many countries adopted
a "wait and sea" attitude.

For some, the fact that Israel has submarines
may torpedo the peace process.

3 – ISRAEL
A) ISRAEL IS REAL

When they talked about strikes and sanctions, some in Israel
aimed at Iraq, others at employers.

An Israeli division of labor:
prophets in Jerusalem,
profits in Tel Aviv.

A peace process may be needed among divided Israelis
and require more than an Oslo-type accord.

A tombstone says, "Here lies an Israeli Prime Minister."
Israeli media says, "The Prime Minister lies."

On the issue of pirate radio stations,
Israeli right-wing parties are on the same wavelength.

In the Promised Land
many promises are not kept.

Calling for early elections in Israel
may open Pandora's ballot box.

If a Prime Minister does not pay attention to social tension,
(s)he may be sent to pension.

A terror campaign
can blow up an election campaign.

It's not easy to read the mind
of the People of the Book.

In Israeli elections some wish the black hats were blackballed.

No Israeli government will be able to bury
the issue of secular cemeteries.

Israel has integrated immigrants from all over the world,
but has not integrated itself yet in the Middle East.

Every week there are lies
in some weeklies.

Every once in a while in Israel
a wind of change blows through a window of opportunity.

The Israeli Supreme Court banned torture by the security
services:
it put an end to persecution by the prosecution.

Some in Israel find it convenient to throw the ball
into the Supreme Court.

In Israel any criticism of the Air Force
is groundless.

Israel is both a state and a nation,
but it prefers the United States to the United Nations.

The Israeli government waits for peace in the region
to declare war on poverty.

Will live coverage of riots with use of live ammunition
save lives?

An Israeli Prime Minister must reach the critical mass of
his government before being criticized by the masses.

An Israeli Minister indicted for sexual harassment[29] needs to
keep abreast of events but not to sit on his bottom line.

Israeli researchers are young.
They work on genes in jeans.

Sometimes the Speaker of the Knesset
can be a loud speaker.

Why do secular girls in Tel Aviv
dress in black like rabbis?

With regard to the religious-secular conflict,
many Israelis wonder how long intolerance will be tolerated.

When the voters have reservations about their leaders,
they make reservations for the next plane.

The Israeli government will get into deep water
if it does not solve the drought issue.

The Israeli Prime Minister often wants to buy time,
but does (s)he know the price to pay?

There are those who aim at a noble peace,
and others at a Nobel Peace Prize.

B) POLITICS, PARTIES AND POLITICIANS

In Israel, everything is political:
as soon as you meet people, you say "Shalom" (peace).

It is easier for a politician to make long sentences about
freedom than to serve a long prison sentence.

Hypocrisy

Some Israeli politicians are judged on their convictions,
others get convictions from judges.

When a politician does not serve the public during his term,
he may serve a term in prison.

If a Prime Minister does not address joblessness,
(s)he may end up jobless.

Some Israeli politicians
are sawing the Party Branch that they are sitting on.

Some political leaders twist facts with their opponents,
while twisting their allies' arms.

In Israel when some politicians are appointed,
others are disappointed.

Israel is probably the only country
where even soccer can be right- or left-wing.[30]

Israeli political parties that result from a split in existing parties
usually call for unity.

As in many countries, Israeli politicians first run for seats,
then when elected, run away from responsibilities.

In most cases those running a party
are accused of ruining it.

When a party leader treats his allies as underdogs,
his party may go to the dogs.

C) NETANYAHU & LIKUD

When Bibi snubbed Bill[31]
Israel paid the bill.

If Area 'C'[32] of the West Bank were named after Netanyahu,
it would be called the 'Bibi C'.

When Bibi was said to kill two birds with one stone,
one wondered whether those were doves or hawks.

The Prime Minister tried to pull some rabbis from his hat.

Once the Russian voters in Israel said, "Nyet to you, Netanyahu."

Bibi or not Bibi, that was the question
asked of the Israeli voters.

Bibi ruled Israel.
Israel ruled him out.

When a leader has not taken enough steps,
he must step down.

A Likud conclusion after the elections:
"the party is finished."

Some activists say Netanyahu didn't do what Likud to save the
party.

There was once a Rabin government.
Later there was a Rabbinate government.

The Ariel Sharon method:
first send the tanks, then the thanks.

In Israeli politics,
you never know where to Begin.[33]

D) BARAK & LABOR

Let's remember that Ehud Barak
came from a military barrack.

It sometimes takes the election of a military man
to prevent civil war.

Israeli democracy still suffers from Labor pains.

No wonder a former chief-of-staff wanted to parachute
his own candidates onto his electoral list.

A dilemma for Barak:

to get the backing of the Knesset,

or to get it off his back.

In Israel the peace camp is not necessarily the Labor camp.

When the Left is right,

the Right is left behind.

The Israeli Left must be judged on its own Meretz.[34]

There was once a Berlin Wall.

Will there be a Beilin[35] Wall in Jerusalem?

4) – THE PALESTINIANS

In the West Bank

they call on Western banks.

Arafat was in a Palestinian state of mind.

After the Jericho casino

a Gaza strip tease?

In Nablus, the population has the blues.

The Palestinians want to be at the negotiating table,

but not in the plate.

A young Palestinian became famous by throwing rocks.
He was a rock star.

The Palestinian people are looking for an identity
while the Israeli authorities confiscate identity cards.

Arab Christians demonstrate during Mass.
Muslim Arabs organize mass demonstrations.

The Intifadah was an occupational hazard.

The Palestinian economy needs checks not checkpoints.

The people of Orient House[36] are disorientated.

A harbor in Gaza
still harbors fears in Israel.

Who wants mullahs in Ramallah?

The Palestinians don't want to give up one inch
of the land they don't have.

Those who give the green light to terrorism
beyond the Green Line[37] will be caught red-handed.

Some attempts to increase Palestinian citrus exports
were fruitless.

Gaza is the land of Hamas, not the Bahamas.

A sign of peace: activists abandon the Molotov cocktail
for the cocktail party.

They found natural gas in Gaza.
This will be a change from tear gas.

When Palestinians are asked to try terrorists,
they sometimes answer, "We'll try."

Most people would prefer the Palestinian State
not to be a Stalinian State.

The Palestinians who thought they could win a war against
Israel are dead wrong.
And dead.

The Intifadah was a *Fatah*[38] *accompli.*

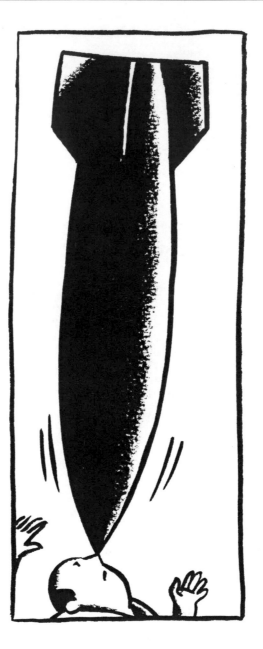

Balance of Forces

A Brave New World Order

(Geneva, New York, 1991-1993)

1 – INTRODUCTION

The world is changing fast. The Cold War is over. The 'Evil Empire'[39] has collapsed. A new map of Europe has emerged. One arms race has stopped. A new proliferation race has begun for weapons of mass destruction, creating even more competition and risks. International institutions, in particular the Geneva-based Conference on Disarmament, have a hard time keeping up with the pace of change and adjusting to new challenges. Here are some more modest testimonies to this discrepancy that inspired one witness in his everyday professional life from 1991 to 1993.

2 – THE 'FORMER SOVIET UNION'

Many used to fear explosions coming from the Soviet Union. After the explosion of the Soviet Union, their fears are even greater.

The dismantlement of the Soviet Union raises the problem
of the dismantlement of its arsenal.

The former Red Army
has the blues.

Star system in Washington.
Czar system in Moscow.

The Communist regime was caught red-handed.

Another name for the former Soviet Union:
Untied Nations.

The right-wing people who never called Russia the Soviet
Union were proven right.

Some naive people think that, because there is a CIS,[40]
there is no more CIA.

A revolution occurred in Eastern Europe: the Czechs now
have checks, Polish people can buy polish, in Hungary
no one is hungry, but in Crimea there is still crime and near
the Black Sea still a black market.

News from some former Soviet Union states.
Good news: they have come out of the state of crisis.
Bad news: they have gone into the state of chaos.

The 'end of History' was announced.
But in the Balkans, it was a return to Prehistory.

3 – A New World Disorder

Some prefer the old world order
to a new world disorder.

Post-Cold War.
Post-Gulf War.
Post-mortem.

The Cold War is over, but hot spots still exist.

Some believe in the force of the law.
Others in the law of force.

In many countries the fear of Moscow
has been replaced by the fear of mosques.

Disarmament agreements once labeled as "historic"
are being made obsolete by the speed of history.

One U.S. administration used to say "Trust but verify."[41]
Another one didn't even trust verification.

Some people regret the old world order.
Should superpowers be put on the list of endangered species?

Some countries align themselves
with the Non-aligned.

The concept of a freeze on armaments
is a remnant of the Cold War.

Paranoia

Ex-German Democratic Republic,[42] Ex-Warsaw Pact, Ex-Soviet
Union, Ex-Yugoslavia, Ex-Czechoslovakia, Ex-Apartheid. . .
Isn't this world ex-citing?

There was the Wall.
Now there is only Wall Street.

4 – NONPROLIFERATION OF WEAPONS OF MASS DESTRUCTION

The logic of nuclear deterrence: it worked among enemies,
it should work among friends; therefore it should be
maintained.

Western countries used to spend money to arm themselves,
now they spend money to disarm others.

The subject of conversion of the military industry
will be the subject of many conversations.

Some countries have been converted
to the conversion of the military industry.

More and more runners want to join the arms race.
Is it still open for entry?

In the area of nonproliferation, big powers sometimes behave
like the reckless parents of unwanted children who, out of
remorse, wish to make birth control compulsory.

The nonproliferation process is like when a few people start
smoking in a non-smoking room: if you don't stop them early
enough, more people will smoke shortly.
(This is why proliferators must be smoked out).

Some regions are threatened by arms transfers.
Arms transfers are threatened by peace.

Some take confidence-building measures,
others arsenal-building measures.

It is better to have arms dealers unemployed
than their arms employed.

While some countries have second thoughts about their
weapons, others do not even think about theirs.

Some lobbies are spending much energy and sparing no effort
to spare military spending.

A sign of technological progress:
smart bombs have replaced dum-dum bullets.

The victims of a missile do not care whether it was a long-,
medium-, or short-range one.

The major arms suppliers can call their insolvent clients
"Dear friends."

Retaliation

Some third-world countries are scared by their population explosion. Others scare their populations with explosions.

Some governments launch disarmament plans.
Others plan the launching of missiles.

The reluctance of some countries to deal with the issue of transparency in armaments is transparent.

It is easier for a "have-not"[43] to become a "have"
than for a "have" to become a "have-not" again.

Some leaders claim that their priority is development.
But they mean the development of weapons.

The generosity of some countries has no limits:
although they renounce weapons of mass destruction,
they keep helping others to make them.

Some countries produce arms.
The United Nations produces reports on arms.

The half-life of some nuclear materials
may be shorter than that of myths about nuclear weapons.

After fearing fall-out from nuclear weapons,
some countries fear the social fall-out of disarmament.

Some governments are still closed
to openness on armaments.

How is it possible to be constructive
regarding weapons of mass destruction?

On arms trade, there can be no trade-offs.

On transfers of high technology,
some countries keep a low profile.

For the military industrial complex,
disarmament is a matter of life and death.

5 – THE CONFERENCE ON DISARMAMENT (CD)

General and complete disarmament is a goal.
The Conference on Disarmament is the goal-keeper.

In the Conference on Disarmament, instead of choosing
between old and new thinking,
some prefer wishful thinking.

In disarmament statements, delegations often mention
cornerstones, milesones, keystones.
Who will cast the first stone at them?

Some delegations still apply the "The answer is no,
what's the question?" policy.

The Threat

The Conference on Disarmament deals with various subjects,
but may be subject to various deals.

Some of the arguments presented in the Conference on
Disarmament are disarming.

There are still divas in disarmament but they often sing the
same song.

Conference on Disarmement (CD) players often play the same
song for the record.

Some delegations to the Conference on Disarmament behave
like drivers who keep their eyes only on the rear-view mirror.
Beware of the crash!

Although the Conference on Disarmament has lost its high
priests,
it continues with its rituals.

What will happen to the Conference on Disarmament if it does
not adjust to the new world?
The same that happens to a woman losing her beauty: nothing.

In a disarmament conference, like in many areas, the best way
to have an opponent agree to your idea is to let him/her believe
that it comes from him/her.

Conference circles may have vicious circles to square.

In a disarmament forum, competition in armaments
is matched by competition in arguments.

In a disarmament conference, the surplus of ideas on
procedure
is usually proportional to the deficit of ideas on substance.

In the area of disarmament, the disappearance of blocs
did not remove all stumbling blocks.

In a disarmament negotiation,
the end-game often justifies the means.

Delegates who deal both with human rights and disarmament
have an easy task:
most of the countries they criticize are the same.

Some delegations express their positions in statements,
others in understatements.

The fact that some chairpersons appoint friends[44]
does not mean that they only have enemies.

The Accord

A few Conference clichés:

a Representative is always distinguished; a cooperation, full; a
skill, diplomatic; a guidance, able; a proposal, constructive; a
discussion, in-depth; an expert, qualified; an interest, great; a
welcome, warm; a gratitude, deep; a work, useful; an idea,
interesting; an initiative, welcome, etc.

The sense of modesty of a chairperson should be encouraged
when (s)he is congratulated
on his/her accession to the chair due to alphabetical order.

The utmost flexibility is displayed by a delegate
who agrees with the two previous speakers
who expressed opposing views.

In an arms control negotiation, meeting the deadline and
breaking the deadlock can prevent deaths.

In a conference, there are bodies, organs, heads (of delegation),
footnotes.
Who said it was not human?

On missile defense,
some countries are on the defensive.

An amendment is often a sentence.
A killer-amendment[45] is a death sentence.

The most vocal supporters of universality and multilateralism
in arms control are usually only guided by their bilateral
relations with their neighbors or opponents.

A secret agenda is better than no agenda at all.

The more a delegation invokes a sense of urgency,
the more it causes delay.

Meetings of Ambassadors can also be meetings of minds.

A head of delegation usually puts his national hat on before
addressing a topic from the top of his head in a brainstorming
meeting.

6 – ANY OTHER BUSINESS

The usual conference agenda item "Any Other Business"
implies that it was preceded by some business.
This is sometimes misleading.

Apart from 'Madam Chairperson', a few suggestions
for politically correct expressions, free of male chauvinism:
gentleperson, brinkpersonship, personkind, personcott,
workpersonship, craftspersonship, personpower, Personhattan,
Un-personned Aerial Vehicle, etc.

Attemps at hair-splitting
can be brushed aside.

A few national oxymorons[46] (no offense meant): British cuisine, French punctuality, Italian precision, American culture, Japanese expansiveness, German flexibility, Russian transparency, Swiss disorder, etc.

Common ground is usually found
with common sense.

Some impatient people would like to replace the step-by-step approach with a leap-by-leap approach.

In most capitals when the Ministry of Defense wants financing the Ministry of Finance is on the defensive.

World affairs are foreign to some diplomats.

In the Foreign Service,
people are used to lip service.

There was a persuasion gap
in the Persian Gulf.

Beating swords into ploughshares
is a double-edged sword.

When the Americans were beating around the bush,
the British had a major problem.[47]

The remnants of Latin civilization:
audio (I hear), *video* (I see), *Volvo*® (I ride).

Many countries could do without foreign AIDS.

In Wall Street, stocks and securities are bought to increase
dividends.
In disarmament, stocks are destroyed to increase security and
peace dividends.

Why does the media always mention "top officials"
and never "bottom officials"?

Was it fair to call Bill Clinton
a Little Rock[48]'n' roll President?

United Kingdom, United States, United Nations, Re-United
Germany, European Union.
What next?

Stargazing

Disarmament And Other Aphorisms For The Guidance Of Arms Control Negotiatiors

(Geneva, New York, 1989-1991)

1 – INTRODUCTION

Diplomats, experts or politicians who discuss arms control matters or negotiate disarmament agreements often do not realize how obscure the language they use may be for the general public, or how rich it can be with double meaning, thanks in particular to the flexibility of English, which has truly become an international idiom.

By standing back, listening with special attention, or attempting to discover a touch of humor in the most serious statements or situations, a modest negotiator with some experience in multilateral forums dared to come up with the following few aphorisms inspired by his professional activities; may they help colleagues or laymen always to serve a good cause without losing contact with reality.

2 – WAR AND PEACE

The end of the Cold War was warmly welcomed.

War: Some like it hot.

The Cold War continued in spite of hot lines.

There is no difference between war and love:
once you start making it, you have to go all the way.

War is only a word. A dirty war is a dirty word.

Some find it easier to lose a battle than to lose face.

It is easier to play war in the Gulf
than to play golf in the war.

The most devastating star wars
are fought in Hollywood.

Despite the fall of the Iron Curtain, some actors would still like
to play war in the European theatre.

3 – ARMS AND WEAPONS

With arms, you can either embrace or kill.

Arm-twisting is not easy in arms control.

In an arms control conference,
the Chair should be called the arm-chair.

After developing weapons of mass destruction,
states will have to start a mass destruction of weapons.

The French word '*détente*'[49] also means 'trigger' (of a weapon).

A heavy bomber cannot be taken lightly.

Nuclear is anything but unclear.

There is a risk of proliferation of measures
designed to curb the proliferation of weapons.

Some want to preserve the arms race, others the human race.

The INF[50] Treaty was the first one to eliminate a whole class of
weapons. It could be called a first-class treaty.

Emptying the missile silos of rich countries
will not necessarily fill the grain silos of poor countries.

4– COUNTRIES

If India joined the Nonproliferation Treaty,[51]
it would be a surprise party.

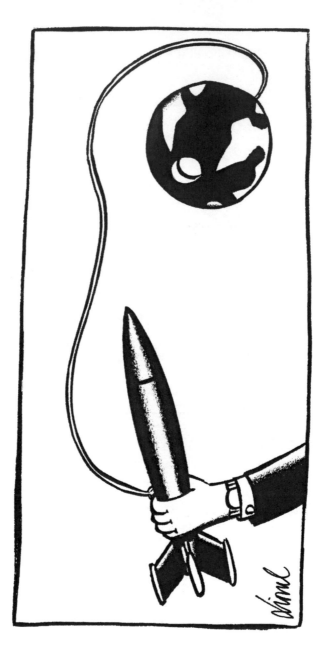

Dangerous Game

In the late seventies, the Soviets intervened in Afghanistan.
Later, they hardly intervened in a plenary meeting.

In the South Pacific, some prefer the best tan to a test ban.[52]

A diplomat from Warsaw was advised to go to London to polish
his English.
He said, "My English is Polish enough."

Having lost all its satellites on Earth,
the Soviet Union tried to preserve its satellites in space.

The fact that, for a long time, the "New World" meant America
does not mean that the New World Order should be "Pax
Americana".

The Berlin Wall has collapsed.
The Chinese Great Wall is still there.

5 – COLORS

Red tape at the White House.
White hope on Red Square.

The fact that some former Red Army bombs can be sold on the
black market
makes some people purple with rage.

Some blueprints are worked out in black and white,
others come out of the blue.

While Western voters gave a green light to Environmentalists,
East European voters gave a red light to Communists.

You may need red rags
to move sacred cows.

6 – NEGOTIATIONS

No wonder there is bargaining in disarmament conferences:
"negotiation" comes from the Latin word meaning "trade".

An agreement on disarmament is always better
than a disagreement on armament.

Some expect instructions from their capital,
others from the Capitol.

A conference room is the only place where a chair does not
stand on the floor
but gives the floor to speakers.

Often, when the floor is open,
mouths are shut.

Any race ends at a finish line with a winner.
How about the arms race?

Infinite War

Instead of sitting in working bodies,
diplomats should sometimes make their bodies work.

For some, the framework may count
more than the work.

A possible new motto for France:
"when you are right,
you are left
alone."

Conventional disarmament sometimes requires
an unconventional approach.

Advice to a delegate going to New York:
"Carpe Per Diem."[53]

A break may either lead to a breakthrough
or to a breakdown.

Judging by their content, some 'non-papers'[54] deserve that
name.

The more warmly a Chairperson or a delegate is thanked for an
initiative, the more severely (s)he should expect to be criticized.

In the field of armaments, you need to take stock
before dealing with stockpiles.

Solitude

Flexibility is often a synonym for indecisiveness.

The absence of "strong feelings"
usually means a total lack of interest.

Although delegates usually are addressed as "distinguished",
most do not try to distinguish themselves from the others.
Some even lack distinction.

Delegates are often exhausted
before the agenda is.

The nuclear-weapon states show their resolution by abstaining
from pushing the button. The non-nuclear states sometimes
push the button to abstain on some resolutions.[55]

Some delegates like talking so much
that they practice double talk.

With regard to naval disarmament,
Western countries are in the same boat.

Delegates who claim that their positions are clear
can be expected to be pretty obscure.

The more comprehensive a Program of Disarmament[56] is,
the more likely it is to remain a program.

Rhetoric

Delegates often spend more time arguing about how to use
their working time than actually using it.

The energy spent by some states in disarming others
is usually proportional to the energy they spend on protecting
their own armaments.

It sometimes takes eggheads
to deal with warheads.

Some international instruments lack harmony.
They need to be played by ear.

Saying that a proposal contains interesting ideas and deserves
careful consideration
is an elegant way of rejecting it.

The START[57] negotiations ended.
Will they start again?

The height of servility for a diplomat:
to write his/her Ambassador's statement
and take notes when (s)he delivers it.

Some heads of delegation work hand in hand, others twist
others' arms, pull others' legs, get cold feet, shoot themselves
in the foot, have big mouths, play it by ear,
or are a pain in the neck.

7 – GOVERNMENTS

Governments are never faced with power shortages.

The winds of change will not let the dust settle.

Military intelligence is not necessarily
always a contradiction.

Shouldn't there be a weather forecast
for the political climate?

Summit meetings give rise to high expectations.

It was easy for some East European diplomats to leave the
Party
for the cocktail party.

Definition of a superpower:
it does not tolerate interference in its internal affairs
anywhere in the world.

Television replaced ideology:
we have entered the era of videology.

Some Ambassadors have a bottom line
but sit on it.

Hierarchy

ADDENDUM

All the authors of the following items are anonymous and the latter are, to my knowledge, unprotected by copyright. I wish both to pay tribute to the actual authors of those items for their sense of humor, and to apologize if readers consider some of them as politically incorrect. Needless to say, I do not approve of any racist or sexist connotation they may sometimes contain.

1) TERMS USED IN MULTILATERAL NEGOTIATIONS AND WHAT THEY USUSALLY MEAN

TERMS USED	WHAT IS USUALLY MEANT
…, or if I may put it another way…	I wish to contradict myself
Perhaps the Chair could explain?	I trust the Chair does not agree with what has been said
I know that these are the views of many	Nobody agrees with this but I will try to push it through anyway

Perhaps we can adjourn for a coffee break?	FROM THE FLOOR: I want to consult other delegations
	FROM THE CHAIR: Delegates appear to be unwilling to discuss this item
…in the spirit of compromise…	I shall repeat what I just said using different words
Speaking off the cuff…	Using prepared text, without showing that I do so…
To the best of my knowledge…	Speaking off the cuff
I wish to enter a reservation	I am stuck
I listened with interest	I took little notice
If I have understood correctly…	I am going to distort what you just said
We note…	We do not agree with what has been said
We note with satisfaction…	We agree with what has been said, but do not intend to do anything about it
We welcome…	We agree with what has been said and might, if pushed, do something at some point
Speaking personally,…	I have rigid instructions
Recognising the importance of…	Some half-witted committee adopted this hare-brained idiocy and we are stuck with it
I have no instructions	I am waiting for instructions
I am waiting for instructions	I have instructions but I will not reveal them until I see which way the wind is blowing

Mr. Chairman, you will surely agree…	Watch your step, Mr. Chairman
I shall be *very* brief	I expect to speak for about 20 minutes
I shall endeavor to be *very* brief	I intend to speak for more 20 minutes
I am confused / I have not understood	I have understood, but do not agree
I do not wish to stand in the way	But I am going to…
Perhaps some flexibility could be shown?	Perhaps other Delegations could come round to our way of thinking?
With respect, Mr. Chairman…	I am going to be disrespectful
With the greatest possible respect, Mr. Chairman…	I am going to be extremely disrespectful
I'm afraid, Mr Chairman, my point cannot be made succinctly	Oh Jesus!
While I have some sympathy with my colleague's remark…	He's talking rubbish…
While I can agree with my colleague up to a point…	He's talking complete rubbish…
My colleague has made a good point, but…	He's talking complete and absolute rubbish…
I wonder if my colleague would care to relate that remark to a somewhat different one he made some minutes ago…	Nice one

What I think my colleague is trying to say is…	I'll twist his words around completely
My colleague has raised the very point I was about to open…	Why didn't I think of that…?
I could be wrong, but…	I know damn well I'm right
If my memory serves me correctly…	I have it chapter and verse in front of me
My Authorities…	The chap in the next office…
My Capital…	The chap in the next office but one…
While English is not my mother tongue…	Why can't the British and Americans be clear?
I haven't had time to study the document in depth	I haven't even opened it
I have studied the paper very carefully.	I glanced through it this morning.
While I have the floor…	I intend to make sure no one else has it…
On a related subject…	I'm changing the subject completely…
On a slightly related subject…	I could even be speaking at another meeting…
It is not for me to comment on that…	But I'm damn well going to…
I honestly cannot improve on what's said…	But I'm going to have a damn good try…
I have no strong feelings…	Only rigid ones…
Whilst I have no wish to go over old ground…	Back to paragraph 1…

I wonder Mr. Chairman, if you could summarize how we stand on this...

I'm afraid, Mr. Chairman, I must leave at four o'clock for another meeting...

I haven't been paying the slightest attention...

See you at the bar

2) BLONDES

Did you hear about the two blondes who froze to death in a drive-in movie?

They went to see "Closed for the Winter."

■

First blonde: "I just took a pregnancy test."

The other: "Were any of the questions difficult?"

■

Why did the blonde resolve to have only three children?

She heard that one child out of every four children born in the world was Chinese.

■

A blonde goes to the local novelty shop and finds a pair of X-ray glasses. She checks them out, and isn't fully convinced, but as usual, the store assistant comes along and closes the deal. On her way home, she puts on her new X-ray glasses and, bingo! She sees everyone in the street naked. She takes them off for a moment, and everyone has their clothes on. Puts the glasses

Echo

back on... everyone is naked! "Cool!" As she arrives back home, she is eager to show her new toy to her husband, but can't find him. She goes up to the bedroom and finds her husband and the young woman from next door naked in bed. She takes the glasses off, and the two are still naked. She put them back on, and they are still naked. "Darn, I just paid fifty bucks for these and they're already broken!"

■

A blonde hurries into the emergency room late one night with the tip of her index finger shot off. "How did this happen?" the emergency room doctor asks her. "Well, I was trying to commit suicide," the blonde replies. "What," sputters the doctor, "you tried to commit suicide by shooting your finger off?" "No, Silly," the blonde says, "first I put the gun to my chest, and I thought, I just paid $6,000 for these breast implants, I'm not shooting myself in the chest." "So then?" asks the doctor. "Then I put the gun in my mouth, and I thought, I just paid $3,000 to get my teeth straightened, I'm not shooting myself in the mouth." "So then?" "Then I put the gun to my ear, and I thought, this is going to make a loud noise. So I put my finger in the other ear before I pulled the trigger."

■

A blonde is driving home after a game and gets caught in a really bad hailstorm. Her car is covered with dents, so the next day she takes it to a repair shop. The shop owner sees that she is a blonde, so he decides to have some fun. He tells her just to go home and blow into the tailpipe really hard, and all the dents would pop out. So, the blonde goes home, gets down on her hands and knees and starts blowing into her tailpipe. Nothing happens. So she blows a little harder, and still nothing happens. Her roommate, another blonde, comes home and says, "What are you doing?" The first blonde tells her how the repairman instructed her to blow into the tailpipe in order to get all the dents to pop out. The roommate rolls her eyes and says, "Uh, like Hello! You need to roll up the windows first."

■

A blonde goes to an eye doctor to have her eyes checked for glasses. The doctor directs her to read various letters with the left eye while covering the right eye. The blonde is so mixed up on which eye is which that the eye doctor, in disgust, takes a paper lunch bag with a hole to see through, covers up the appropriate eye, and asks her to read the letters. As he does so, he notices the blonde has tears streaming down her face. "Look," says the doctor, "there's no need to get emotional about getting glasses." "I know," agrees the blonde, "but I kind of had my heart set on wire frames."

■

A blonde is shopping at a department store and comes across a silver thermos. She is quite fascinated by it, so she picks it up and brings it over to the clerk to ask what it is. The clerk says, "Why, that's a thermos. . . it keeps things hot and some things cold." "Wow," says the blonde, "that's amazing… I'm going to buy it!" So she buys the thermos and takes it to work the next day. Her boss sees it on her desk. "What's that," he asks? "Why,

that's a thermos. . . it keeps hot things hot and cold things cold,"
she replies. Her boss inquires, "What do you have in it?" The
blonde replies, "Two popsicles, and some coffee."

■

A blonde lady is stopped by a blonde police officer for a minor
traffic violation. "May I see your license please?" The lady,
"License? What does it look like?" The officer: "One of those little
plastic thingies with your photo on it." The lady proceeds to
rummage through her bag, and triumphantly produces her
compact mirror and hands it over to the police officer. The officer
snaps open the compact, looks into it and says, "If you told me that
you were a police officer right away, I wouldn't have stopped you."

■

Two blondes in the shower: "Pass me some other shampoo,
please." "But you have some near you…" "I know, but this one is
for dry hair and mine is wet…"

■

Two blondes are riding a bicycle. One gets off the bike and
starts letting some air out of the tires. "What are you doing?" asks
the other one. "My seat is too high", answers the other.

■

Two blondes are watching the full moon, one asks: "Do you
think there is life up there?" "Of course," the other one answers,
"there is light!"

■

A blonde wants to sell her old car but does not succeed
because it totals 250,000 miles. She asks her friend for advice.

The brunette says, "Are you ready to do something illegal?" "Of course, I want to sell it at any price." "So go to see my friend Tony the mechanic. He's going to set the odometer back to 50,000 miles." The blonde goes to see Tony, who resets the odometer to 50,000 miles. A few days later, the brunette asks the blonde, "Did you sell your car?" "Are you crazy? Now that the odometer has only 50,000 miles, I'm keeping it!"

■

Two blondes are in a car; and a bird drops guano on the windshield. One says, "We'll have to wipe it." The other answers: "Too late, it is too far already!"

■

Two blondes walk into a building… you'd think at least one of them would have seen it.

■

A blonde, wanting to earn some money, decides to hire herself out as a handyman-type and starts canvassing a wealthy neighborhood. She goes to the front door of the first house and asks the owner if he has any jobs for her to do. "Well, you can paint my porch. How much will you charge?" The blonde replies, "How about fifty dollars?" The man agrees and tells her that the paint and ladders that she might need are in the garage. The man's wife, inside the house, hears the conversation and says to her husband, "Does she realize that the porch goes all the way around the house?" The man replies, "She should. She was standing on the porch." A short time later, the blonde comes to the door to collect her money. "You're finished already?" he asks.

"Yes," the blonde answers, "and I had paint left over, so I gave it two coats." Impressed, the man reaches in his pocket for the fifty dollars. "And by the way," the blonde adds, "that's not a Porch, it's a Ferrari."

■

Blonde Calendar

January – Took new scarf back to store because it was too tight.

February – Fired from pharmacy job for failing to print labels because bottles won't fit in typewriter.

March – Got excited... finished jigsaw puzzle in six months... box said "two to four years!"

April – Trapped on escalator for hours... power went out!!!

May – Tried to make Kool-Aid®58... eight cups of water won't fit into those little packets!!!

June – Tried to go water skiing... couldn't find a lake with a slope.

July – Lost breast stroke swimming competition... learned later, other swimmers cheated, they used their arms!!!

August – Got locked out of car in rain storm... car swamped, because top was down.

September – The capital of California is "C"... isn't it?

October – Hate M&M's®59... they are so hard to peel.

November – Baked turkey for four and a half days... instructions said one hour per pound and I weigh 108!!!

December – Couldn't call 911... because there's no "eleven" button on the phone!!!

What a year!!

■

Two Chimps and a Blonde

A blonde lady car driver is about two hours from San Diego when she is flagged down by a man whose truck has broken down. The man walks up to the car and asks, "Are you going to San Diego?" "Why, Yes I am," answers the blonde, "do you need a lift?" "Not for me. I'll probably be spending the next three hours fixing my truck. My problem is I've got two chimpanzees in the back, and they have to be taken to the San Diego Zoo. They're a bit stressed already so I don't want to keep them on the road all day. Could you possibly take them to the zoo for me? I'll give you a hundred dollars for your trouble." "I'd be happy to," says the blonde. So the two chimpanzees are ushered into the back seat of the blonde's car and carefully strapped into their seat belts. Off they go. Five hours later, the truck driver is driving through the heart of San Diego when suddenly he is horrified! There is the blonde walking down the street and holding hands with the two chimps. With a screech of brakes he pulls off the road and runs over to the blonde. "What the heck are you doing here?" he demands, "I gave you money to take these chimpanzees to the zoo." "Yes Sir, I know you did," says the blonde, "but we had money left over— so now we're going to Sea World."

■

Blonde and Frog

A lovely and very sexy blonde goes into her local pet shop in search of an exotic pet. As she looks about the store, she notices a box full of frogs. The sign says, "Sex Frogs! Only twenty dollars each! Comes with complete instructions." The blonde excitedly looks around to see if anybody's watching her. She whispers softly to the man behind the counter, "I'll take one." As the man packages the frog, he quietly says to her, "Just follow the instructions." The blonde nods, grabs the box, and is quickly on her way home. As soon as she closes the door to her apartment, she opens the instructions and reads them very carefully. She does exactly what is specified:

1. Put some nice satin sheets on your bed.
2. Take a nice warm bubble bath.
3. Splash on some nice perfume.
4. Slip into a very sexy nightie.
5. Light a pair of candles by the bed.
6. Put on a CD with some very soft classical music playing quietly in the background.
7. Slip into bed and place the frog beside you. The frog will do what he has been trained to do.

She quickly gets into bed with the frog and, to her surprise, nothing happens. The blonde is very disappointed and quite upset at this point. She re-reads the instructions and notices at the bottom of the paper it says, "If you have any problems or questions, please call the pet store and speak to the man that sold the frog to you." So the blonde calls the pet shop. The man says, "I'll be right over." Within minutes, the man is ringing her doorbell. The blonde welcomes him in and says, "See, I've done everything according to the instructions. The stupid frog just sits there." The man, looking very concerned, picks up the frog, stares into its eyes and says very sternly, "Look, I'm only going to show you how to do this one more time!"

3) MEN AND WOMEN, MARRIAGE, COUPLES, ETC.

E-Mail

A couple from Minneapolis decides to go to Florida for a long weekend to thaw out during one particularly icy winter. They plan to stay at the very same hotel where they spent their honeymoon twenty years ago. Because both have jobs, they find it difficult coordinating their travel schedules. It is decided that the husband would fly to Florida on a Thursday, and his wife would follow him the next day. Upon arriving as planned, the husband checks into the hotel. In his room there is a computer, so he decides to send his wife an e-mail back in Minneapolis. However, he accidentally leaves out one letter in her address and sends the e-mail without realizing his error. In Houston, a widow has just returned from her husband's funeral. The dearly departed was a minister of many years who had been called home to glory following a heart attack. The widow checks her e-mail, expecting messages from relatives and friends. Upon reading the first message, she faints. The widow's son rushes into the room, finds his mother on the floor, and sees the computer screen which reads:

To: My Loving Wife –

Subject: I've Arrived.

I know you are surprised to hear from me. They have computers here now and you are allowed to send e-mails to your loved ones. I've just arrived and have been checked in. I see that everything has been prepared for your arrival tomorrow. Looking forward to seeing you then! Hope your journey is as uneventful as mine was. P.S. Sure is hot down here!

Genie

A husband takes his young wife to play her first game of golf The wife promptly hacks her first shot right through the window of the biggest house adjacent to the course. The husband cringes, "I warned you to be careful! Now we'll have to go up there, find the owner, apologize and see how much your lousy drive is going to cost us." So the couple walks up to the house and knocks on the door. A warm voice says, "Come on in." When they open the door they see the damage that was done: glass all over the place, and a broken antique bottle lying on its side near the broken window. A handsome man reclining on the couch asks, "Are you the people that broke my window?" "Uh. . . yeah, sir. We sure are sorry about that," the husband replies. "Oh, no apology is necessary. Actually I want to thank you. You see, I'm a genie, and I've been trapped in that bottle for a thousand years. Now that you've released me, I'm allowed to grant three wishes. I'll give you each one wish, but if you don't mind, I'll keep the last one for myself." "Wow, that's great!" the husband says. He ponders a moment and blurts out, "I'd like a million dollars a year for the rest of my life." "No problem," says the genie. "You've got it, it's the least I can do. And I'll guarantee you a long, healthy life!" "And now you, young lady, what do you want?" the genie asks. "I'd like to own a gorgeous home complete with servants in every country in the world," she says. "Consider it done," the genie replies. "And your homes will always be safe from fire, burglary, and natural disasters!" "And now," the couple asks in unison, "what's your wish, genie?" "Well, since I've been trapped in that bottle and haven't been with a woman in more than a thousand years, my wish is to sleep with your wife." The husband looks at his wife and says, "Gee, honey, you know we both now have a fortune, and all those houses. What do you think?" She mulls it over for a few moments and says, "You know, you're right. Considering our good fortune, I guess I wouldn't mind, but what about you, honey?" "You know I love you sweetheart," says the husband. "I'd do the same for you!" So the genie and the woman go upstairs where they spend the rest of the afternoon enjoying each other. The genie is insatiable. After about three hours of total fun, the genie rolls over and looks directly into her eyes and asks, "How old are you and your husband?" "Why, we're both 35," she responds breathlessly. "Really?! Thirty-five years old and both of you still believe in genies?"

Attrition

Bill is not having a good day on the golf course. After he missed a twelve-inch putt, his partner asks him what the problem is. "It's the wife," says Bill. "As you know, she's taken up golf, and since she's been playing she's cut my sex down to once a week." "Well you should think yourself lucky," says his partner, "she's cut some of us out altogether!"

Marriage Stories

A typical macho man marries a typical good-looking lady and after the wedding, he lays down the following rules: "I'll be home when I want, if I want, and at what time I want – and I don't expect any hassle from you. I expect a great dinner to be on the table unless I tell you that I won't be home for dinner. I'll go hunting, fishing, boozing, and card-playing when I want with my buddies and don't you give me a hard time about it. Those are my rules. Any comments?" His new bride says, "No, that's fine with me. Just understand that there will be sex here at seven o'clock every night... whether you're here or not."

■

A husband and a wife have a bitter quarrel on the day of their fortieth wedding anniversary. The husband yells, "When you die, I'm getting you a headstone that reads, 'Here Lies My Wife – Cold As Ever.' "Yeah?" she replies. "When you die, I'm getting you a headstone that reads, 'Here Lies My Husband Stiff At Last.'"

■

A husband, who is a doctor, and his wife are having a fight at the breakfast table. The husband gets up in a rage and says, "And you are no good in bed either," and storms out of the house. After sometime he realizes he was nasty and decides to make amends and rings her up. She comes to the phone after many rings, and the irritated husband says, "What took you so long to answer the phone?" She says, "I was in bed." "In bed this early, doing what?" "Getting a second opinion!"

■

A man has six children and is very proud of his achievement. He is so proud of himself, that he starts calling his wife "Mother of Six" in spite of her objections. One night, they go to a party. The man decides that it's time to go home and wants to find out if his wife is ready to leave as well. He shouts at the top of his voice, "Shall we go home Mother of Six?" His wife, irritated by her husband's lack of discretion shouts right back, "Anytime you're ready, Father of Four."

■

God may have created man before woman but there is always a rough draft before the masterpiece.

■

Two guys are discussing trends in sex, marriage, and values. Stu says, "I didn't sleep with my wife before we got married, did you?" Leroy replies, "I'm not sure, what was her maiden name?"

■

A little boy goes up to his father and asks, "Dad, where did all of my intelligence come from?" The father replies, "Well, son, you must have gotten it from your mother, because I still have mine."

■

"Mr. Clark, I have reviewed this case very carefully," the divorce court judge says, "and I've decided to give your wife a thousand a week." "That's very fair, your honor," the husband says. "And every now and then I'll try to send her a few bucks myself."

■

A doctor examines a woman, takes the husband aside, and says, "I don't like the looks of your wife at all." "Me neither doc," says the husband. "But she's a great cook and really good with the kids."

■

An old man goes to the Wizard to ask him if he can remove a curse he has been living with for the last forty years. The Wizard says, "Maybe, but you will have to tell me the exact words that were used to put the curse on you." The old man says without hesitation, "I now pronounce you man and wife."

■

A husband and wife go to a psychiatrist after fifteen years of marriage. The psychiatrist asks them what the problem is and the wife goes into a tirade listing every problem they have ever had in the fifteen years they've been married. She goes on and on and on. Finally, the psychiatrist gets up, goes around the desk, embraces the woman and kisses her passionately, rips off her clothes and makes mad passionate love to her. Needless to say, the woman shuts up and sits quietly with a very satisfied daze. The psychiatrist turns to the husband and says, "That is what your wife needs at least three times a week. Can you do that?" The husband thinks for a moment and replies, "Well, I can get her here Monday and Wednesday, but Friday I play golf."

■

A wife is making a breakfast of fried eggs for her husband. Suddenly, her husband bursts into the kitchen. "Careful," he says,

"CAREFUL! Put in some more butter! Oh my GOSH! You're cooking too many at once. TOO MANY! Turn them! TURN THEM NOW! We need more butter. Oh my GOSH! WHERE are we going to get MORE BUTTER? They're going to STICK! Careful, CAREFUL. I said be CAREFUL! You NEVER listen to me when you're cooking! Never! Turn them! Hurry up! Are you CRAZY? Have you LOST your mind? Don't forget to salt them. You know you always forget to salt them. Use the salt. USE THE SALT! THE SALT!" The wife stares at him. "What in the world is wrong with you? You think I don't know how to fry a couple of eggs?" The husband calmly replies, "I wanted to show you what it feels like when I'm driving."

■

One day, a man comes home and is greeted by his wife dressed in a very sexy nightie. "Tie me up," she purrs, "and you can do anything you want." So he ties her up and goes to play golf.

Wife versus Husband

A couple drives down a country road for several miles, not saying a word. An earlier discussion has led to an argument and neither of them wants to concede their position. As they pass a barnyard of mules, goats, and pigs, the husband asks sarcastically, "Relatives of yours?" "Yep," the wife replies, "in-laws."

■

A husband reads an article to his wife about how many words women use a day. . . "Thirty thousand to a man's fifteen thousand." The wife replies, "The reason has to be because we have to repeat everything to men..." The husband then turned to his wife and asks, "What?"

■

A man says to his wife one day, "I don't know how you can be so stupid and so beautiful all at the same time." The wife responds, "Allow me to explain. God made me beautiful so you would be attracted to me; God made me stupid so I would be attracted to you!"

■

A man and his wife are having an argument about who should brew the coffee each morning. The wife says, "You should do it, because you get up first, and then we don't have to wait as long to get our coffee." The husband says, "You are in charge of cooking around here and you should do it, because that is your job, and I can just wait for my coffee." Wife replies, "No, you should do it, and besides, it is in the Bible that the man should do the coffee." Husband replies, "I can't believe that, show me." So she fetches the Bible, and opens the New Testament and shows him at the top of several pages, that it indeed says. . . "HEBREWS."

■

A man and his wife are having some problems at home and giving each other the silent treatment. Suddenly, the man realizes that the next day he needs his wife to wake him at 5:00 A.M. for an early morning business flight. Not wanting to be the first to break the silence (and lose), he writes on a piece of paper, "Please wake me at 5:00 A.M." He leaves it where he knows she would find it. The next morning, the man wakes up, only to discover it is 9:00 A.M. and he has missed his flight. Furious, he is about to go and see why his wife hasn't wakened him, when he notices a piece of paper by the bed. The paper says, "It is 5:00 A.M. Wake up."

■

A man and his wife are dining at a table in a posh restaurant, and the husband keeps staring at a drunken lady swigging her drink as she sits alone at a nearby table. The wife asks, "Do you know her?" "Yes," sighs the husband, "She's my ex-girlfriend. I understand she took to drinking right after we split up seven years ago, and I hear she hasn't been sober since." "My God!" says the wife, "Who would think a person could go on celebrating that long?"

■

A guy goes to the supermarket and notices an attractive woman waving at him. He waves back and says hello. He's rather taken aback because he can't place exactly where he knows her. So he says, "Do you know me?" She replies, "I think you're the father of one of my kids." Now his mind travels back to the only time he has ever been unfaithful to his wife and says, "My God, are you the stripper from my bachelor party that I made love to on the pool table with all my buddies watching?" She looks into his eyes and says calmly, "No, I'm your son's teacher."

Marriage and Maths

ROMANCE MATHEMATICS

Smart man + smart woman = romance

Smart man + dumb woman = affair

Dumb man + smart woman = marriage

Dumb man + dumb woman = pregnancy

SHOPPING MATH

A man will pay twenty dollars for a ten-dollar item he needs.

A woman will pay ten dollars for a twenty-dollar item that she doesn't need.

GENERAL EQUATIONS AND STATISTICS

A woman worries about the future until she gets a husband.

A man never worries about the future until he gets a wife.

A successful man is one who makes more money than his wife can spend.

A successful woman is one who can find such a man.

HAPPINESS

To be happy with a man, you must understand him a lot and love him a little.

To be happy with a woman, you must love her a lot and not try to understand her at all.

LONGEVITY

Married men live longer than single men do, but married men are a lot more willing to die.

PROPENSITY TO CHANGE

A woman marries a man expecting he will change, but he doesn't.

A man marries a woman expecting that she won't change, and she does.

TECHNICAL DISCUSSION
A woman has the last word in any argument.
Anything a man says after that is the beginning of a new argument.

HOW TO STOP PEOPLE FROM BUGGING YOU ABOUT
GETTING MARRIED
Old aunts used to come up to me at weddings, poking me in the ribs and cackling, telling me, "You're next." They stopped after I started doing the same thing to them at funerals.

Husband Mart

A store that sells husbands has just opened in Ottawa, Canada, where a woman may go to choose a husband from among many men. The store is comprised of six floors, and the men increase in positive attributes as the shopper ascends the flights. There is, however, a catch. As you open the door to any floor you may choose a man from that floor, but if you go up a floor, you cannot go back down except to exit the building. So a woman goes to the shopping center to find a husband.

On the first floor the sign on the door reads: "Floor 1 – These men have jobs." The woman reads the sign and says to herself, "Well, that's better than my last boyfriend, but I wonder what's further up?" So up she goes.

The second floor sign reads: "Floor 2 – These men have jobs and love kids" The woman remarks to herself, "That's great, but I wonder what's further up?" And up she goes again.

The third floor sign reads: "Floor 3 – "These men have jobs, love kids, and are extremely good looking." "Hmmm, better" she says. "But I wonder what's upstairs?"

The fourth floor sign reads: "Floor 4 – These men have jobs, love kids, are extremely good looking, and help with the housework." "Wow!" exclaims the woman, "very tempting. BUT, there must be further up!" And again she heads up another flight.

The fifth floor sign reads: "Floor 5 – These men have jobs, love kids, are extremely good looking, help with the housework, and have a strong romantic streak." "Oh, mercy me! But just think. . . what must be awaiting me further on?" So up to the sixth floor she goes.

The sixth floor sign reads: "Floor 6 – You are visitor 3,456,789,012 to this floor. There are no men on this floor. This floor exists solely as proof that women are impossible to please. Thank you for shopping at Husband Mart and have a nice day."

Warship

After a nine-month deployment, the aircraft carrier USS *Oriskany* is finally inching up to the pier at her homeport in Alameda when the Captain notices a sailor on the flight deck gesturing wildly with semaphore flags. He then notices an attractive young woman standing on top of a stationwagon, also waving semaphore flags. Always concerned about security and never having seen anything like this, the Captain barks at his Bridge Signalman, "What message are those two people sending?" The Signalman concentrates intently and soon reports, "Sir, he is sending FOXTROT-FOXTROT and she is sending ECHO-FOXTROT." Not having any clue as to what these messages could mean, the Captain dispatches an armed Marine to escort the Sailor back to the Bridge. The sailor arrives, out of breath from running up the many ladders to the bridge, and salutes smartly. "Seaman Endicott reporting as ordered, Sir!" "Endicott", shouts the Captain, "Who is that woman on the pier and why are you exchanging signals FF and EF?" "Sir. That's my wife, Sir. She wants to eat first."

Would You Remarry?

A husband and wife are sitting quietly in bed reading when the wife looks over at him and asks the question. . .

WIFE: "What would you do if I died? Would you get married again?"

HUSBAND: "Definitely not!"

WIFE: "Why not? Don't you like being married?"

HUSBAND: "Of course I do."

WIFE: "Then why wouldn't you remarry?"

HUSBAND: "Okay, okay, I'd get married again."

WIFE: "You would?" (with a hurt look)

HUSBAND: (makes audible groan)

WIFE: "Would you live in our house?"

HUSBAND: "Sure, it's a great house."

WIFE: "Would you sleep with her in our bed?"

HUSBAND: "Where else would we sleep?"

WIFE: "Would you let her drive my car?"

HUSBAND: "Probably, it is almost new."

WIFE: "Would you replace my pictures with hers?"

HUSBAND: "That would seem like the proper thing to do."

WIFE: "Would you give her my jewellery?"

HUSBAND: "No, I'm sure she'd want her own."

WIFE: "Would she use my golf clubs?"

HUSBAND: "No, she's left-handed."

WIFE: – silence –

HUSBAND: "sh*t."

Red Skelton's Tips for a Happy Marriage

(Red Skelton was a comedian in the United States back in the days when entertainment wasn't so raunchy)

Two times a week, we go to a nice restaurant, have a little beverage, then comes good food and companionship. She goes on Tuesdays, I go on Fridays.

We also sleep in separate beds. Hers is in Ontario and mine is in Tucson.

I take my wife everywhere, but she keeps finding her way back.

I asked my wife where she wanted to go for our anniversary: "Somewhere I haven't been in a long time!" she said. So I suggested the kitchen.

We always hold hands. If I let go, she shops.

She has an electric blender, electric toaster, and electric bread maker. Then she said, "There are too many gadgets and no place to sit down!" So I bought her an electric chair.

My wife told me the car wasn't running well because there was water in the engine. I asked where the car was, she told me, "In the Lake."

She got a mudpack and looked great for two days. Then the mud fell off.

She ran after the garbage truck, yelling, "Am I too late for the garbage?" The driver said, "No, jump in!"

Remember: marriage is the number one cause of divorce. Statistically, 100% of all divorces start with marriage.

I married Miss Right. I just didn't know her first name was Always.

I haven't spoken to my wife in eighteen months. I don't like to interrupt her.

The last fight was my fault. My wife asked, "What's on the TV?" I said, "Dust."

The Good Life

A man is walking down the street when he is accosted by a particularly dirty and shabby-looking homeless man who asks him for a couple of dollars for dinner. The man takes out his wallet, extracts ten dollars and asks, "If I give you this money, will you buy some beer with it instead of dinner?" "No, I had to stop drinking years ago," the homeless man replies. "Will you use it to go fishing instead of buying food?" the man asks. "No, I don't waste time fishing," the homeless man says. "I need to spend all my time trying to stay alive." "Will you spend this on greens fees at a golf course instead of food?" the man asked. "Are you NUTS!" replies the homeless man. "I haven't played golf in twenty years!" "Will you spend the money on a woman in the red light district instead of food?" the man asks. "What disease would I get for ten lousy bucks?" exclaims the homeless man. "Well," says the man, "I'm not going to give you the money. Instead, I'm going to take you home for a terrific dinner cooked by my wife." The homeless man is astounded. "Won't your wife be furious with you for doing that? I know I'm dirty, and I probably smell pretty disgusting." The man replies, "That's okay. It's important for her to see what a man looks like after he has given up beer, fishing, golf, and sex."

Of Frogs and Men (and Women)

So most MEN think they're smarter than the female species...

A woman is out golfing one day when she hits the ball into the woods. She goes to retrieve it and finds a frog in a trap. The frog says to her, "If you release me from this trap, I will grant you three wishes." The woman frees the frog, and the frog says, "Thank you, but I failed to mention that there was a condition to your wishes." "Whatever you wish for, your husband will get times ten!" The woman tells the frog that is fine with her, and for her first wish, she wants to become the most beautiful woman in the world. The frog warns her, "You do realize that this wish will also make your husband the most handsome man in the world, an Adonis whom women will flock to." The woman replies, "That's okay, because I will be the most beautiful woman and he will have eyes only for me." With that, the frog makes her the most beautiful woman in the world.

For her second wish, she wants to be the richest woman in the world. The frog says, "That will also make your husband the richest man in the world." "He will be ten times richer than you." The woman confides, "That's okay, because what's mine is his and what's his is mine." With that, she instantly becomes the richest woman in the world.

The frog then inquires about the woman's third wish, to which she answers, "I'd like a mild heart attack." Moral of the story: women are clever. Don't mess with them.

Attention female readers: this is the end of the joke for you. Stop here and continue feeling good about yourselves.
Male readers only: please read on...

The man has a heart attack ten times milder than his wife.

Moral of the story: women like to think they're really smart. Best to let them think that way and just sit back and order another beer from the kitchen.

P.S. If you are a woman and are still reading this, it only goes to show that women never listen.

Be Careful What You Wish For

A married couple in their early sixties are out celebrating their thirty-fifth wedding anniversary in a quiet, romantic, little restaurant. Suddenly, a tiny yet beautiful fairy appears at their table and says, "For being such an exemplary married couple and for being faithful to each other for all this time, I will grant you each a wish." "Ooh, I want to travel around the world with my darling husband" says the wife. The fairy waves her magic stick and abracadabra! Two tickets for the QM2 luxury liner appear in the wife's hands. Now it is the husband's turn. He thinks for a moment and says, "Well this is all very romantic, but an opportunity like this only occurs once in a lifetime, so I'm sorry my love, but my wish is to have a wife thirty years younger than me." The wife and the fairy are deeply disappointed, but a wish is a wish. So, the fairy makes a circle with her magic wand and abracadabra! The husband becomes ninety-two years old.

The moral of this story: men might be ungrateful idiots, but fairies are... FEMALE!!

Men!

A woman's remark: Okay, Okay, it finally all makes sense now.
. . I never looked at it this way before:

MENtal illness,

MENstrual cramps,

MENtal breakdown,

MENopause,

GUYnecologist,

and when we have real trouble, it's a HISterectomy.

Ever notice how all of women's problems start with MEN?

Fishing Trip

A woman is in bed with her lover who happens to be her husband's best friend. They make love for hours, and afterwards, while they're just laying there, the phone rings. Since it is the woman's house, she picks up the receiver. Her lover looks at her and listens, only hearing her side of the conversation. She speaks in a cheery voice, "Hello? Oh, hi! I'm so glad that you called. Really? That's wonderful. I am so happy for you. That sounds terrific. Great! Thanks. Okay. Bye." She hangs up the telephone, and her lover asks, "Who was that?" "Oh," she replies, "that was my husband telling me all about the wonderful time he's having with you on his fishing trip."

Deciphering Men's Speech Patterns

(From a Woman's Viewpoint)

1. "I can't find it."

   MEANS: it didn't fall into my outstretched hands, so I am completely clueless.

2. "That's women's work."

   MEANS: it's difficult, dirty, and thankless.

3. "Will you marry me?"

   MEANS: both of my roommates have moved out, I can't find the washer, and there's no peanutbutter left.

4. "It's a guy thing."

   MEANS: there's no rational thought pattern connected with it, and you have no chance at all of making it logical.

5. "Can I help with dinner?"

   MEANS: why isn't it already on the table?

6. "It would take too long to explain."

   MEANS: I have no idea how it works.

7. "I'm getting more exercise lately."

   MEANS: the batteries in the remote are dead.

8. "We're going to be late."

MEANS: I have a legitimate reason for driving like a maniac.

9   "Take a break, honey, you're working too hard."

MEANS: I can't hear the game over the vacuum cleaner.

10. "That's interesting dear."

MEANS: are you still talking?

11. "Honey, we don't need material things to prove our love."

MEANS: I forgot our anniversary again.

12. "You expect too much from me."

MEANS: you expect me to stay awake?

13. "It's really a good movie."

MEANS: it's got guns, knives, fast cars, and naked women.

14. "You know how bad my memory is."

MEANS: I remember the words to the theme song of F-Troop, the address of the first girl I kissed, and the vehicle identification number of every car I've ever owned, but I forgot your birthday.

15. "I was just thinking about you, and got you these roses."

MEANS: the girl selling them on the corner was a real babe, and was wearing a thong bikini.

16. "Oh, don't fuss, I just cut myself, it's no big deal."

MEANS: I have actually severed a limb, but will bleed to death before I admit I'm hurt.

17. "Hey, I've got reasons for what I'm doing."

MEANS: what did you catch me at?

18. "She's one of those rabid feminists."

MEANS: she refused to make my coffee.

19. "I heard you."

MEANS: I haven't the foggiest clue what you just said, and hope I can fake it well enough, so that you don't spend the next three days yelling at me.

20. "You know I could never love anyone else."

MEANS: I am used to the way YOU yell at me, and realize it could be worse.

21. "You really look terrific in that outfit."

MEANS: please don't try on one more outfit, I'm starving.

22. "I brought you a present."

MEANS: it was free ice scraper night at the ball/hockey game.

23. "I missed you."

MEANS: I can't find my sock drawer, the kids are hungry, and we're out of toilet paper.

24. "I'm not lost, I know exactly where we are."

MEANS: no one will ever see us alive again.

25. "This relationship is getting too serious."

MEANS: I like you almost as much as I like my truck.

26. "I don't need to read the instructions."

MEANS: I am perfectly capable of screwing it up without printed help.

Female Comebacks or Ways to Turn Men Down

Man: "Haven't I seen you someplace before?"

Woman: "yes, that's why I don't go there anymore."

Man: "Is this seat empty?"

Woman: "yes, and this one will be if you sit down."

Man: "Your place or mine?"

Woman: "both, you go to yours, and I'll go to mine."

Man: "Hey baby, what's your sign?"

Woman: "do not enter."

Man: "How do you like your eggs in the morning?"

Woman: "unfertilized."

Man: "Your body is like a temple."

Woman: "sorry, there are no services today."

Man: "I would go to the end of the world for you!"

Woman: "but would you stay there?"

Man: "If I could see you naked, I'd die happy."

Woman: "if I saw you naked, I'd probably die laughing."

Man: "Can I buy you a drink?"

Woman: "actually I'd rather have the money."

Man: "I'm a photographer. I've been looking for a face like yours."
Woman: "I'm a plastic surgeon. I've been looking for a face like yours."

Man: "Hi! Didn't we go on a date once? Or was it twice?"
Woman: "must've been once. I never make the same mistake twice."

Man: "How did you get to be so beautiful?"
Woman: "I must've been given your share."

Man: "Will you go out with me this Saturday?"
Woman: "sorry, this Saturday I'm having a headache."

Man: "Your face must turn a few heads."
Woman: "and your face must turn a few stomachs."

Man: "Go on, don't be shy. Ask me out."
Woman: "Okay, get out."

Man: "I think I could make you very happy."
Woman: "why, are you leaving?"

Man: "What would you say if I asked you to marry me?"
Woman: "nothing, I can't talk and laugh at the same time."

Man: "Can I have your name?"
Woman: "why, don't you already have one?"

Man: "Shall we go see a movie?"
Woman: "I've already seen one."

Man: "Where have you been all my life?"
Woman: "hiding from you."

Man: "Where have you been all my life?"
Woman: "where I'll be the rest of your life – in your wildest dreams."

Men Strike Back!

How many men does it take to open a beer?
None. It should be opened when she brings it.

Why is a Laundromat® a really bad place to pick up a woman?
Because a woman who can't even afford a washing machine will probably never be able to support you.

Why do women have smaller feet than men?
It's one of those "evolutionary things" that allows them to stand closer to the kitchen sink.

How do you know when a woman is about to say something smart?
When she starts a sentence with "A man once told me..."

How do you fix a woman's watch?
You don't. There is a clock on the oven.

If your dog is barking at the back door and your wife is yelling at the front door, who do you let in first?

The dog, of course. He'll shut up once you let him in.

What's worse than a Male Chauvinist Pig?

A woman who won't do what she's told.

Scientists have discovered a food that diminishes a woman's sex drive by ninety percent.

It's called a Wedding Cake.

Why do men die before their wives?

They want to.

Women will never be equal to men until they can walk down the street with a bald head and a beer gut, and still think they are sexy.

In the beginning, God created the Earth and rested.

Then God created Man and rested.

Then God created Woman.

Since then, neither God nor Man has rested.

How to Keep a Woman Happy?

It's not difficult. All you have to do is to be:

1.   friend,
2.   a companion,
3.   a lover,

4. a brother,

5. a father,

6. a master,

7. a chef,

8. an electrician

9. a carpenter,

10. a plumber,

11. a mechanic,

12. a decorator,

13. a stylist,

14. a sexologist,

15. a gynaecologist,

16. a psychologist,

17. a pest exterminator,

18. a psychiatrist,

19. a healer,

20. a good listener,

21. an organizer,

22. a good father,

23. very clean,

24. sympathetic,

25. athletic,

26. warm,

27. attentive,

28. gallant,

29. intelligent,

30. funny,

31. creative,

32. tender,

33. strong,

34. understanding,

35. tolerant,

36. prudent,

37. ambitious,

38. capable,

39. courageous,

40. determined,

41. true,

42. dependable,

43. passionate,

WITHOUT FORGETTING TO:

44. give her compliments regularly,

45. love shopping,

46. be honest,

47. be very rich,

48. not stress her out,

49. not look at other girls,

AND AT THE SAME TIME, YOU MUST ALSO:

50. give her lots of attention, but expect little yourself,

51. give her lots of time, especially time for herself,

52. give her lots of space, never worrying about where she goes.

IT IS VERY IMPORTANT

53. never to forget

a. birthdays,

b. anniversaries,

c. arrangements she makes.

How to Keep a Man Happy?

All you have to do is:

1. leave him in peace,

2. feed him well,

3. and let him have the remote control.

Knowing Your Partner

While attending a Marriage Encounter Weekend, Bill and his wife Carol are listening to the instructor declare, "It is essential that husbands and wives know the things that are important to each other." He addresses the men, "Can you name and describe your wife's favorite flower?" Bill leans over, touches Carol's arm gently and whispers, "Self-raising, isn't it?" And thus begins Bill's life of celibacy.

Infidelity

A salesman is testifying in his divorce proceedings against his wife. "Please describe," says his attorney, "the incident that first caused you to entertain suspicions as to your wife's infidelity." "Well, I'm pretty much on the road all week," the man testifies. "So naturally when I am home, I'm attentive to the wife." One Sunday morning," he continues, "we were in the midst of some pretty heavy lovemaking when the old lady in the apartment next door pounded on the wall and yelled, 'Can't you at least stop all that racket on the weekends?"

Burial

A man and his ever-nagging wife went on vacation to Jerusalem. While they were there, the wife passes away. The undertaker tells the husband, "You can have her shipped home for five grand, or you can bury her here, in the Holy Land, for one hundred and fifty dollars." The man thinks about it and tells him he just wants her shipped home. The undertaker asks, "Why would you spend all that money to ship your wife home, when it would be wonderful to be buried here and you would spend only one fifty?" The man replies, "Long ago I have been told, a man died here, was buried here, and three days later he rose from the dead. I just can't take that chance."

Pharmacy

A lady walks into a drug store and tells the pharmacist she needs some cyanide. The pharmacist says, "Why in the world do you need cyanide?" The lady then explains she needs it to poison her husband. The pharmacist's eyes get big and he says, "Lord have mercy, I can't give you cyanide to kill your husband! That's against the law! I'll lose my license, they'll throw both of us in jail and all kinds of bad things will happen! Absolutely not, you can NOT have any cyanide!" Then the lady reaches into her purse and pulls out a picture of her husband in bed with the pharmacist's wife. The pharmacist looks at the picture and replies, "Well now, you didn't tell me you had a prescription."

Pest Control

My husband works as a service technician for a large exterminating company. One of the rules of the company is that he has to confirm each appointment by phone the night before his service call to that household. One evening he made such a call, and when a man answered the phone, he said, "Hi, this is Gary from the Pest Control Company. Your wife phoned us." There was a long silence, and then my husband heard the man on the other end say, "Honey, it's for you. . . someone wants to talk to you about your relatives."

Home, Sweet Home

A man staggers home late after another evening with his drinking buddies. Shoes in left hand to avoid waking his wife, he tiptoes as quietly as he can toward the stairs leading to the upstairs bedroom, but misjudges the bottom step in the darkened entryway. As he catches himself by grabbing the banister, his body swings around and he lands heavily on his rump. A whisky bottle in each back pocket breaks and makes the landing especially painful. Managing to suppress a yelp, the man springs up, pulls down his pants, and examines his lacerated and bleeding cheeks in the mirror of a nearby hallway, then manages to find a large full box of Band-Aids®60 and proceeds to place a patch as best he can on each place he sees blood. After hiding the now almost empty box, he manages to shuffle and stumble his way to bed. In the morning, the man awakes with searing pain in head and butt and sees his wife staring at him from across the room. She says, "You were drunk again last night!" Forcing himself to ignore his agony, he looks meekly at her and replies, "Now, honey, why would you say such a mean thing?" "Well," she said, "it could be the open front door, it could be the glass at the bottom of the stairs, it could be the drops of blood trailing through the house, it could be your bloodshot eyes, but, mostly.... it's all those Band-Aids® stuck on the downstairs mirror!"

Barbie® Doll

One day a father gets out of work and on his way home he remembers that it's his daughter's birthday. He pulls over to a toy store and asks the salesperson, "How much is the Barbie® on the display window?" The salesperson answers, "Which one? We have:

Workout Barbie® for $19.95,

Shopping Barbie® for $19.95,

Beach Barbie® for $19.95,

Disco Barbie® for $19.95,

Divorced Barbie® for $265.95."

The amazed father asks, "What? Why is the Divorced Barbie® $265.95 and the others only $19.95?"

The salesperson annoyingly answers, "Sir, Divorced Barbie® comes with:

Ken®'s Car,

Ken®'s Boat,

Ken®'s Furniture,

Ken®'s Computer and...

Ken®'s House!"

Sentence

An eighty-year-old woman is arrested for shoplifting. When she goes before the judge he asks her, "What did you steal?" She replies, "A can of peaches." The judge asks her why she stole them and she replies that she was hungry. The judge then asks her how many peaches were in the can. She replies, "Six." The judge then says, "I will give you six days in jail." Before the judge could actually pronounce the punishment, the woman's husband speaks up and asks the judge if he could say something, and the judge agrees. The husband says, "She also stole a can of peas."

How to Tell the Sex of a Fly

A woman walks into the kitchen to find her husband stalking around with a fly swatter. "What are you doing?" she asks. "Hunting flies" he responds. "Oh. Killing any?" "Yep, three males, two females," he replies. Intrigued, she asks, "How can you tell?" He responds, "Three were on a beer can, two were on the phone."

Men are like....

Weather: nothing can be done to change them.

Blenders: you need one, but you're not quite sure why.

Chocolate: sweet, smooth, and head right for your hips.

Commercials: you can't believe a word they say.

Department Stores: their clothes are always half-off.

Government Bonds: they take sooooooooo long to mature.

Mascara: they usually run at the first sign of emotion.

Popcorn: they satisfy you, but only for a little while.

Snowstorms: you never know when they're coming, how many inches you'll get or how long it will last.

Lava Lamps: fun to look at, but not very bright.

Parking Spots: all the good ones are taken, the rest are handicapped.

Our Chemical Make Up

Element Name: WOMAN.

Symbol: Wo.

Atomic Weight: don't even go there!!

Physical Properties: generally round in form, boils at nothing and may freeze at any time, melts whenever treated properly. Very bitter if not used well.

Chemical Properties: yery active. Highly unstable, especially when left alone. Possesses strong affinity to gold, silver, platinum, and precious stones. Able to absorb great amounts of exotic food. Turns slightly green when placed next to a better specimen. Usage: highly ornamental. An extremely good catalyst for dispersion of wealth. Probably the most powerful income reducing agent known.

Caution: highly explosive in inexperienced hands.

Element Name: MAN.

Symbol: Xy.

Atomic Weight: 180 +/- 50.

Physical Properties: fairly dense and sometimes flaky. Difficult to find pure sample.

Chemical Properties: attempts to bond with Wo any chance it can get. Also tends to form strong bonds with itself. Becomes explosive when mixed with Kd (element: child) for prolonged period of time. Neutralize by saturating with alcohol.

Usage: none known. Possibly good methane source. Good samples are able to produce large quantities on command.

Caution: in the absence of Wo, this element rapidly decomposes and begins to smell.

Horse Races

A guy is sitting quietly reading his paper when his wife walks up behind him and whackes him on the head with a magazine. "What was that for?" he asks. "That was for the piece of paper in your pants pocket with the name Laura Lou written on it," she replies. "Two weeks ago when I went to the races, Laura Lou was the name of one of the horses I bet on," he explains. "Oh honey, I'm sorry," she says. "I should have known there was a good explanation." "Three days later he is watching a ballgame on TV when she walks up and hits him in the head again, this time with the iron skillet, which knocks him out cold. When he comes to, he asks, "What the hell was that for?" She replies, "Your horse called."

Divorce

A married couple is driving along a highway doing a steady sixty miles (ninety-six km) per hour. The wife is behind the wheel. Her husband suddenly looks across at her and speaks in a clear voice. "I know we've been married for twenty years, but I want a divorce." The wife says nothing, keeps looking at the road ahead but slowly increases her speed to sixty-five mph (104 kph). The husband speaks again. "I don't want you to try and talk me out of it," he says, "because I've been having an affair with your best friend, and she's a far better lover than you are." Again the wife stays quiet, but grips the steering wheel more tightly and slowly increases the speed to seventy-five mph (120 kph). He pushes his luck. "I want the house," he says insistently. Up to eighty mph (128 kph). "I want the car, too," he continues. Now eighty-five mph (136 kph). "And," he says, "I'll have the bank accounts, all the credit cards, and the boat!" The car slowly starts veering toward a massive concrete bridge. This makes him nervous, so he asks her, "Isn't there anything you want?" The wife at last replies in a quiet and controlled voice. "No, I've got everything I need," she says. "Oh, really," he inquires, "so what have you got?" Just before they slam into the wall at eighty-five mph (136 kph), the wife turns to him and smiles. "The airbag."

The Boss

The boss is complaining in a staff meeting that he isn't getting any respect. The next day, he brings a small sign that reads: "I'm the Boss!" He then tapes it to his office door. Later that day when he returns from lunch, he finds that someone has taped a note to the sign that says: "Your wife called, she wants her sign back!"

A Secret of Long Marriage

A couple is celebrating their golden wedding anniversary. Their domestic tranquility has long been the talk of the town. "What a peaceful and loving couple." A local newspaper reporter is inquiring as to the secret of their long and happy marriage. "Well, it dates back to our honeymoon," explains the man. "We visited the Grand Canyon and took a trip down to the bottom on the canyon by horse. We hadn't gone too far when my wife's horse stumbled. My wife says, "That's once." We proceed a little further and the horse stumbles again. Once more my wife says, "That's twice." We haven't gone a half-mile when the horse stumbles the third time. My wife quietly removes a revolver from her purse and shoots the horse dead. I start an angry protest over her treatment of the horse; while I am shouting, she looks at me, and says, "That's once." And we lived happily ever after."

Mid-life Crisis

When I was married twenty-five years, I took a look at my wife one day and said, "Honey, twenty-five years ago, we had a cheap apartment, a cheap car, slept on a sofa bed, and watched a ten-inch black-and-white TV, but I got to sleep every night with a hot twenty-five-year old blonde. Now, we have a nice house, nice car, big bed and plasma screen TV, but I'm sleeping with a fifty-year old woman. It seems to me that you are not holding up your side of things." My wife is a very reasonable woman. She told me to go out and find a hot twenty-five year old blonde, and she would make sure that I would once again be living in a cheap apartment, driv-

ing a cheap car, sleeping on a sofa bed. Aren't older women great?
They really know how to solve your mid-life crises.

Communication

Three fastest ways of communication in the world:

a. tele-phone.

b. tele-vision.

c. tell-a-woman.

You still want faster?

d. Tell her not to tell anyone.

More Quotes on Marriage

I recently read that love is entirely a matter of chemistry.
That must be why my wife treats me like toxic waste.
(David Bissonette)

When a man steals your wife, there is no better revenge
than to let him keep her.
(Sacha Guitry)

After marriage, husband and wife become two sides of a coin;
they just can't face each other, but still they stay together.
(Hemant Joshi)

Woman inspires us to great things, and prevents us from
achieving them.
(Alexandre Dumas)

The great question. . . which I have not been able
to answer. . . is: "What does a woman want?"
(*Sigmund Freud*)

I had some words with my wife, and she had some
paragraphs with me.
(*Anonymous*)

I don't worry about terrorism. I was married for two years.
(*Sam Kinison*)

There's a way of transferring funds that is even faster than
electronic banking. It's called marriage.
(*James Holt McGavran*)

I've had bad luck with both my wives. The first one left me,
and the second one didn't.
(*Patrick Murray*)

Two secrets to keep your marriage brimming:
1. Whenever you're wrong, admit it.
2. Whenever you're right, shut up.
(*Nash*)

The most effective way to remember your wife's birthday is to
forget it once...
(*Anonymous*)

You know what I did before I married? Anything I wanted to.
(Henny Youngman)

A good wife always forgives her husband when she's wrong.
(Milton Berle)

Marriage is the only war where one sleeps with the enemy.
(Anonymous)

A man inserted an ad in the classifieds: "Wife wanted."
Next day he received a hundred letters.
They all said the same thing: "you can have mine."
(Anonymous)

First Guy (proudly): "My wife's an angel!"
Second Guy: "You're lucky, mine's still alive."
(Anonymous)

More Marriage Aphorisms

(Unknown author[s])
I stayed in love with the same woman for forty-nine years.
If my wife knew it, she'd kill me.

Someone stole my credit card. But I won't report it:
Any burglar would spend less than my wife.

My wife stayed at the beauty parlor for two hours.
But it was for a quote.

What do women have once a month that lasts a couple of days?
Their husband's pay.

Apart from their physical differences, how can you tell a naked
man from a naked woman? The man kept his socks on.

What's the difference between a man and a can of cat food?
In the cat food there's heart and brain.

A neuron arrives at a man's brain and finds no one. Another one
comes and asks, "What are you doing here, we're all down
there?"

Why does a woman marrying a man put a ring on his finger?
To give him some value.

Why is a man's psychoanalysis shorter than a woman's?
Because it's about going back to childhood, and men are still
there.

Why does it take millions of sperm cells to fertilize a
female egg cell? Because sperm cells are male and refuse to ask
for their way around.

Why do men always run after women without wanting to marry
them? For the same reason that dogs always run after cars
without wanting to drive them.

What's the difference between a man and a cat?

None, they both are scared of vacuum cleaners.

A nurse to a mother who just gave birth to a baby:

"Your baby is an angel; once in bed he keeps still."

The mother says, "Just like his father."

A woman calls her husband:

"I spent two weeks in a diet clinic and I lost half my weight."

The husband replies, "There are still two weeks left."

A man asks a librarian for a book entitled "Man, the Strong

Sex."

The librarian says. "Science-fiction's in the basement."

A soon-to-be father to his wife: "If the baby looks like you, it

will be fantastic."His wife retorts, "If the baby looks like you,

it will be a miracle."

4) LAWYERS

Once, in Dublin, a solicitor came up to a barrister to beg a subscription towards the funeral expenses of a brother solicitor who had died in distressed circumstances. The barrister at once tendered a pound note. "Oh, I only want a shilling from each contributor" says the solicitor. "Take it, my dear fellow," replies the barrister. "And while you're at it, bury twenty of them!"

■

The local United Way[61] office realizes that it had never received a donation from the town's most successful lawyer. A local volunteer calls to sollicite his donation, saying, "Our research shows that even though your annual income is over a million dollars, you do not give one penny to charity. Wouldn't you like to give back to your community through The United Way?" The lawyer thinks for a moment and says, "First, did your research show that my mother is dying after a long, painful illness and has huge medical bills far beyond her ability to pay?" Embarrassed, the United Way rep mumbles, "Uh, no." "Secondly, that my brother, a disabled veteran, is blind and confined to a wheelchair and is unable to support his wife and six children?" The stricken United Way rep begins to stammer an apology but is cut off. "Thirdly, that my sister's husband died in a dreadful traffic accident?", the lawyer's voice is rising in indignation, "She was left penniless with a mortgage and three children?" The humiliated United Way rep, completely beaten, says simply, "I had no idea." The lawyer then says, "...and if I don't give any money to THEM, why should I give any to you?"

■

A lawyer finds out he has an inoperable brain tumor. It's so large that they have to do a brain transplant. His doctor gives him a choice of available brains. There's a jar of rocket scientist brains for ten dollars an ounce, a jar of regular scientist brains for fifteen dollars an ounce, and a jar of lawyer brains for the sum of eight-hundred dollars an ounce. The outraged lawyer says, "This is a ripoff! How come the lawyer brains are so damned expensive?" The doctor replies, "Do you know how many lawyers it takes to get an ounce of brains?"

■

"You're a high-priced lawyer! If I give you five hundred dollars, will you answer two questions for me?" Absolutely! What's the second question?"

■

A surgeon, an architect, and a lawyer are having a heated barroom discussion concerning which of their professions is actually the oldest profession. The surgeon says, "Surgery IS the oldest profession. God took a rib from Adam to create Eve and you can't go back further than that." The architect says, "Hold on! In fact, God was the first architect when he created the world out of chaos in seven days, and you can't go back any further than THAT!" The lawyer puffs his cigar and says, "Gentlemen, Gentlemen. . . who do you think created the CHAOS??!!"

■

The Los Angeles Police Department (LAPD), the FBI, and the CIA are all trying to prove that they are the best at apprehending criminals. The President decides to give them a test. He releases a rabbit into a forest and each of them has to catch it. The CIA goes in. They place animal informants throughout the forest. They question all plant and mineral witnesses. After three months of extensive investigations they conclude that rabbits do not exist. The FBI goes in. After two weeks with no leads they burn the forest, killing everything in it, including the rabbit, and they make no apologies. The rabbit had it coming. The LAPD goes in. They come out two hours later with a badly beaten bear. The bear is yelling, "Okay! Okay! I'm a rabbit! I'm a rabbit!"

■

An old man is on his death bed. He wants badly to take all his money with him. He calls his priest, his doctor, and his lawyer to his bedside. "Here's thirty thousand dollars in cash to be held by each of you. I trust you to put this in my coffin when I die so I can take all my money with me." At the funeral, each man puts an envelope in the coffin. Riding away in a limousine, the priest suddenly breaks into tears and confesses that he has only put twenty thousand dollars into the envelope because he needed ten thousand for a new baptistery. "Well, since we're confiding in each other," says the doctor. "I only put ten thousand in the envelope because we need a new machine at the hospital which costs twenty thousand." The lawyer is aghast. "I'm ashamed of both of you," he exclaims. "I want it known that when I put my envelope in that coffin, it held my personal check for the full thirty thousand dollars."

■

It was so cold last week that I saw several lawyers with their hands in their own pockets.

■

As the lawyer wakes up after surgery, he says, "Why are all the blinds drawn?" The doctor answers: "There's a big fire across the street, and we didn't want you to think the operation was a failure."

■

Two lawyers walking through the woods spot a vicious-looking bear. The first lawyer immediately opens his briefcase, pulls out a pair of sneakers, and starts putting them on. The second lawyer looks at him and says, "You're crazy! You'll never be able to outrun that bear!" "I don't have to," the first lawyer replies. "I only have to outrun you."

■

Q: How was copper wire invented?

A: Two lawyers were arguing over a penny.

■

A doctor and a lawyer in two cars collide on a country road. The lawyer, seeing that the doctor is a little shaken up, helps him from the car and offers him a drink from his hip flask. The doctor accepts and hands the flask back to the lawyer, who closes it and puts it away. "Aren't you going to have a drink yourself?" asks the doctor. "Sure; after the police leave," replies the lawyer.

■

At the height of a political corruption trial, the prosecuting attorney attacks a witness. "Isn't it true," he bellows, "that you accepted five thousand dollars to compromise this case?" The witness stares out the window as though he hasn't heard the question. "Isn't it true that you accepted five thousand dollars to compromise this case?" the lawyer repeats. The witness still does not respond. Finally, the judge leans over and says, "Sir, please answer the question." "Oh," the startled witness says, "I thought he was talking to you."

■

Two law partners leave their office and go to lunch. In the middle of lunch the junior partner slaps his forehead. "Damn," he says. "I forgot to lock the office safe before we left." His partner replies, "What are you worried about? We're both here."

■

An Amish man named Smith is injured when he and his horse are struck by a car at an intersection. Smith sues the driver. In court, he is cross-examined by the driver's lawyer. Lawyer: "Mr. Smith, you've told us all about your injuries. But according to the accident report, you told the investigating officer at the scene that you were not injured at all?" Smith: "Well, let me explain. When the officer arrived at the scene, he first looked at my horse. He said "Looks like he has a broken leg," and then he took out his gun and shot the horse. He then came up to me and asked me how I was doing. I of course immediately said "I'm fine!"

■

What is the difference between a tick and a lawyer? A tick falls off of you when you die.

■

Why does the law society prohibit sex between lawyers and their clients? To prevent clients from being billed twice for essentially the same service.

■

What do you call a lawyer who doesn't chase ambulances? Retired.

■

How many lawyers does it take to change a light bulb? Six. One to change the bulb and five to write the environmental impact statement.

■

What do you call a smiling, sober, courteous, person at a bar association convention? The caterer.

■

Why are lawyers like nuclear weapons? If one side has one, the other side has to get one. Once launched, they cannot be recalled. When they land, they screw up everything forever.

■

Many years ago, a junior partner in a firm is sent to a far-away state to represent a long-term client accused of robbery. After days of trial, the case is won, the client acquitted, and released. Excited about his success, the attorney telegraphs the firm: "Justice prevailed." The senior partner replies in haste, "Appeal immediately."

■

Lawyers should never ask a witness a question if they are not prepared for the answer. In a trial, a Southern U.S. small-town prosecuting attorney calls this first witness, a grandmotherly, elderly woman, to the stand. He approaches her and asks, "Mrs. Jones, do you know me?" She responds "Why, yes I do know you Mr. Williams. I have known you since you were a young boy, and, frankly, you have been a big disappointment to me. You lie, you cheat on your wife, and you manipulate people and talk about them behind their backs. You think you are a big shot when you haven't got the brains to realize you never will amount to anything more than a two-bit paper pusher. Yes, I know you." The lawyer is stunned! Not knowing what else to do, he points across the room and asks, "Mrs. Jones, do you know the defense attorney?" She again replies, "Why yes, I do. I have known Mr. Bradley since he was a youngster too. He is lazy, bigoted, and has a drinking problem. He can't build a normal relationship with anyone and his law practice is one of the worst in the entire State. Not to mention he cheated on his wife with three different women. One of them was your wife. Yes, I know him." The defense attorney almost dies. The judge asks both to approach the bench, and in a very quiet voice, says, "If either one of you bastards asks her if she knows me, I'll send you to the electric chair."

5) UNDERSTANDING ENGINEERS

To the optimist, the glass is half full.

To the pessimist, the glass is half empty.

To the engineer, the glass is twice as big as it needs to be.

■

A pastor, a doctor, and an engineer are waiting one morning for a particularly slow group of golfers. The engineer fumes, "What's with these guys? We must have been waiting for fifteen minutes!" The doctor chimes in, "I don't know, but I've never seen such ineptitude!" The pastor says, "Hey, here comes the greens keeper. Let's have a word with him." "Hi, George! Say, what's with that group ahead of us? They're rather slow, aren't they?" The greens keeper replies, "Oh, yes, that's a group of blind fire-fighters. They lost their sight saving our clubhouse from a fire last year, so we always let them play for free anytime." The group is silent for a moment. The pastor says, "That's so sad. I think I will say a special prayer for them tonight." The doctor says, "Good idea. And I'm going to contact my ophthalmologist buddy and see if there's anything he can do for them." The engineer says, "Why can't these guys play at night?"

■

Normal people believe that if it ain't broke, don't fix it. Engineers believe that if it ain't broke, it doesn't have enough features yet.

■

An architect, an artist, and an engineer are discussing whether it is better to spend time with the wife or a mistress. The architect says he enjoyed time with his wife, building a solid foundation for an enduring relationship. The artist says he enjoyed time with his mistress, because of the passion and mystery he found there. The engineer says, "I like both." "Both?" "Yeah. If you have a wife and a mistress, they will each assume you are spending time with the other woman, and you can go to the lab and get some work done."

■

An engineer is crossing a road one-day when a frog calls out to him and says, "If you kiss me, I'll turn into a beautiful princess." He bends over, picks up the frog, and puts it in his pocket. The frog speaks up again and said, "If you kiss me and turn me back into a beautiful princess, I will stay with you for one week. "The engineer takes the frog out of his pocket, smiles at it, and returns it to the pocket. The frog then cries out, "If you kiss me and turn me back into a princess, I'll stay with you and do ANYTHING you want." Again the engineer takes the frog out, smiles at it, and puts it back into his pocket. Finally, the frog asks, "What is the matter with you? I've told you I'm a beautiful princess, and that I'll stay with you for a week and do anything you want. Why won't you kiss me?" The engineer replies, "Look, I'm an engineer. I don't have time for a girlfriend, but a talking frog, now that's cool."

■

What is the difference between mechanical engineers and civil engineers? Mechanical engineers build weapons and civil engineers build targets.

■

The graduate with a science degree asks, "Why does it work?"

The graduate with an engineering degree asks, "How does it work?"

The graduate with an accounting degree asks, "How much will it cost?"

The graduate with an arts degree asks, "Do you want fries with that?"

■

Three engineering students were gathered together discussing who must have designed the human body. One says, "It was a mechanical engineer. Just look at all the joints." Another says, "No, it was an electrical engineer. The nervous system has many thousands of electrical connections." The last one says, "No, actually it has to have been a civil engineer. Who else would run a toxic waste pipeline through a recreational area?"

■

An engineer dies and reports to Hell. Pretty soon, the engineer becomes dissatisfied with the level of comfort in Hell, and starts designing and building improvements. After a while, they've got air conditioning and flush toilets and elevators, and the engineer is a pretty popular guy. One day God calls Satan up on the telephone and says with a sneer, "So, how's it going down there in Hell?" Satan replies, "Hey things are going great. We've got air conditioning and flush toilets and elevators, and there's no telling what this engineer is going to come up with next." God replies, "What??? You've got an engineer? That's a mistake – he should never have gone down there; send him up here." Satan says, "No way. I like having an engineer on the staff, and I'm keeping him." God says, "Send him back up here or I'll sue." Satan laughs and answers, "Yeah, right. And just where are you going to get a lawyer?"

6) QUOTES

ALLEGEDLY GENUINE QUOTES BY GEORGE W. BUSH

(Authenticity unverified)

"The vast majority of our imports come from outside the country."

"If we don't succeed, we run the risk of failure."

"One word sums up probably the responsibility of any Governor, and that one word is 'to be prepared'."

"I have made good judgments in the past. I have made good judgments in the future."

"The future will be better tomorrow."

"We're going to have the best educated American people in the world."

"I stand by all the misstatements that I've made."

"We have a firm commitment to NATO, we are a part of NATO. We have a firm commitment to Europe. We are a part of Europe."

"Public speaking is very easy."

"A low voter turnout is an indication of fewer people going to the polls."

"We are ready for any unforeseen event that may or may not occur."

"For NASA, space is still a high priority."

"Quite frankly, teachers are the only profession that teach
our children."

"It isn't pollution that's harming the environment.
It's the impurities in our air and water that are doing it."

"It's time for the human race to enter the solar system."

Famous and Infamous Quotes

(Compiled by Unknown Author)

"I once had a rose named after me and I was very flattered.
But I was not pleased to read the description in the catalogue:
'No good in a bed, but fine up against a wall'."
(Eleanor Roosevelt)

"Last week I stated this woman was the ugliest woman I had
ever seen. I have since been visited by her sister and now wish
to withdraw that statement."
(Mark Twain)

"The secret of a good sermon is to have a good beginning and a
good ending; and have the two as close together as possible."
(George Burns)

"Santa Claus has the right idea: visit people only once a year."
(Victor Borge)

"Be careful about reading health books.
You may die of a misprint."
(*Mark Twain*)

"What would men be without women?
Scarce, sir. . . mighty scarce."
(*Mark Twain*)

"My wife is a sex object. Every time I ask for sex, she objects."
(*Les Dawson*)

"By all means marry: if you get a good wife, you'll become
happy; if you get a bad one, you'll become a philosopher."
(*Socrates*)

"I was married by a judge.
I should have asked for a jury."
(*Groucho Marx*)

"My wife has a slight impediment in her speech.
Every now and then she stops talking to breathe."
(*Jimmy Durante*)

"The male is a domestic animal which, if treated with firmness
and kindness, can be trained to do most things."
(*Jilly Cooper*)

"I never hated a man enough to give his diamonds back."
(Zsa Zsa Gabor)

"Don't go around saying the world owes you a living.
The world owes you nothing. It was here first."
(Mark Twain)

"My luck is so bad that if I bought a cemetery, people would
stop dying."
(Ed Furgol)

"Money can't buy you happiness,
but it does bring you a more pleasant form of misery."
(Spike Milligan)

"What's the use of happiness? It can't buy you money."
(Henny Youngman)

"I am opposed to millionaires, but it would be dangerous to
offer me the position."
(Mark Twain)

"Until I was thirteen, I thought my name was 'shut up'."
(Joe Namath)

"Youth would be an ideal state if it came a little later in life."
(Herbert Henry Asquith)

"A woman drove me to drink. . .
and I hadn't even the courtesy to thank her."
(*W. C. Fields*)

"I never drink water because of the disgusting things
that fish do in it."
(*W. C. Fields*)

"It takes only one drink to get me drunk. The trouble is, I can't
remember if it's the thirteenth or the fourteenth."
(*George Burns*)

"We could certainly slow the ageing process down if it had to
work its way through Congress."
(*Unknown*)

"Don't worry about avoiding temptation. . .
As you grow older, it will avoid you."
(*Unknown*)

"Maybe it's true that life begins at fifty. But. . . everything else
starts to wear out, fall out, or spread out."
(*Unknown*)

"Doctor to patient: 'I have good news and bad news.
The good news is that you are not a hypochondriac.'"
(*Unknown*)

"The cardiologist's diet:
If it tastes good. . . spit it out."
(*Unknown*)

"By the time a man is wise enough to watch his step, he's too
old to go anywhere."
(*Unknown*)

"It's hard to be nostalgic when you can't remember anything."
(*Unknown*)

"Sex is one of the nine reasons for incarnation.
The other eight are unimportant."
(*George Burns*)

"Hockey is a sport for white men. Basketball is a sport for
black men.
Golf is a sport for white men dressed like black pimps."
(*Tiger Woods*)

"My mother never saw the irony in calling me a son-of-a-bitch."
(*Jack Nicholson*)

"Having sex is like playing bridge. If you don't have a good
partner, you'd better have a good hand."
(*Woody Allen*)

"Bigamy is having one wife too many.

Monogamy is the same."

(Oscar Wilde)

"A bottle in front of me is better than a frontal lobotomy."

(Unknown)

Will Rogers

Will Rogers, an American cowboy-humourist and philan-thropist, who died in a plane crash with Wylie Post in 1935, was probably the greatest political sage the United States has ever known. Enjoy the following remarks he made.

1. Never slap a man who's chewing tobacco.

2. Never kick a cow chip on a hot day.

3. There are two theories to arguing with a woman. . . neither works.

4. Never miss a good chance to shut up.

5. Always drink upstream from the herd.

6. If you find yourself in a hole, stop digging.

7. The quickest way to double your money is to fold it and put it back in your pocket.

8. There are three kinds of men: the ones that learn by reading. The few who learn by observation. The rest of them have to pee on the electric fence and find out for themselves.

9. Good judgment comes from experience, and a lot of that comes from bad judgment.

10.   If you're riding' ahead of the herd, take a look back every now and then to make sure it's still there.

11.   Lettin' the cat outta the bag is a whole lot easier'n put it back in.

12.   After eating an entire bull, a mountain lion felt so good he started roaring. He kept it up until a hunter came along and shot him. The moral: 'When you're full of bull, keep your mouth shut.'

Great Quotes by Great Ladies

"Inside every older lady is a younger lady – wondering what the hell happened."
(*Cora Harvey Armstrong*)

"The hardest years in life are those between ten and seventy."
(*Helen Hayes* – at 73)

"Things are going to get a lot worse before they get worse."
(*Lily Tomlin*)

"Laugh and the world laughs with you.
Cry and you cry with your girlfriends."
(*Laurie Kuslansky*)

"Old age ain't no place for sissies."
(*Bette Davis*)

"A man's got to do what a man's got to do.
A woman must do what he can't."
(*Rhonda Hansome*)

"The phrase 'working mother' is redundant."
(*Jane Sellman*)

"Every time I close the door on reality, it comes in through the windows."
(*Jennifer Unlimited*)

"Whatever women must do they must do twice as well as men to be thought half as good. Luckily, this is not difficult."
(*Charlotte Whitton*)

"Thirty-five is when you finally get your head together and your body starts falling apart."
(*Caryn Leschen*)

"I try to take one day at a time – but sometimes several days attack me at once."
(*Jennifer Unlimited*)

"If you can't be a good example – then you'll just have to be a horrible warning."
(*Catherine II*)

"I'm not offended by all the dumb blonde jokes because I know
I'm not dumb and I'm also not blonde."
(*Dolly Parton*)

"If high heels were so wonderful, men
would still be wearing them."
(*Sue Grafton*)

"When women are depressed they either eat or go shopping.
Men invade another country."
(*Alyne Boosler*)

"Behind every successful man is a surprised woman."
(*Maryon Pearson*)

"In politics, if you want anything said, ask a man.
If you want anything done, ask a woman."
(*Margaret Thatcher*)

"I have yet to hear a man ask for advice on how to combine
marriage and a career."
(*Gloria Steinem*)

"I am a housekeeper.
Every time I leave a man, I keep his house."
(*Zsa Zsa Gabor*)

"Nobody can make you feel inferior without your permission."
(*Eleanor Roosevelt*)

Smart Quotes

(*Authenticity Unverified*)

Question: "If you could live forever, would you and why?"
Answer: "I would not live forever, because we should not live forever, because if we were supposed to live forever, then we would live forever, but we cannot live forever, which is why I would not live forever."
(*Miss America 1995 from Alabama Heather Whitestone*)

"Whenever I watch TV and see those poor starving kids all over the world, I can't help but cry. I mean I'd love to be skinny like that, but not with all those flies and death and stuff."
(*Popular Pop Singer Mariah Carey*)

"Smoking kills. If you're killed, you've lost a very important part of your life."
(*Model, movie and TV actress Brooke Shields, during an interview to become Spokesperson for federal anti-smoking campaign.*)

"I've never had major knee surgery on any other part of my body."
(*University of Kentucky Basketball Forward Winston Bennett*)

"Outside of the killings, Washington has one of the lowest
crime rates in the country."
(*Washington D.C. Mayor Marion Barry*)

"I'm not going to have some reporters pawing through our
papers. We are the President."
(*First Lady Hillary Clinton, commenting on the release of
subpoenaed documents*)

"That lowdown scoundrel deserves to be kicked to death by a
jackass,
and I'm just the one to do it."
(*A congressional candidate in Texas*)

"Half this game is ninety percent mental."
(*Philadelphia Phillies Manager Danny Ozark*)

"We are ready for any unforeseen event that may
or may not occur."
(*Vice President Al Gore*)

"I love California: I practically grew up in Phoenix."
(*Vice President Dan Quayle*)

"We've got to pause and ask ourselves, 'How much clean air do
we need?'"
(*Chrysler Chairman and CEO Lee Iacocca*)

"The word 'genius' isn't applicable in football.

A genius is a guy like Norman Einstein."

(NFL Quarterback and Sports Analyst Joe Theisman)

"We don't necessarily discriminate.

We simply exclude certain types of people."

(Reserve Officers' Training Corps Instructor

Colonel Gerald Wellman)

"Traditionally, most of Australia's imports come from overseas."

(Former Australian Cabinet Minister Keppel Enderbery)

"Your food stamps will be stopped effective March 1992

because we received notice that you passed away.

May God bless you. You may reapply if there is a

change in your circumstances."

(Greenville, South Carolina,

Department of Social Services)

"If somebody has a bad heart, they can plug this jack in at

night as they go to bed and it will monitor their heart

throughout the night. And the next morning, when they wake

up dead, there'll be a record."

(Federal Communications Commission Chairman

Mark S. Fowler)

Quotes by Coluche

*(Coluche was a French comedian and humorist,
who died in 1984 after having founded a chain of charity
restaurants for poor people – Translation from French by the
author of this book)*

All mushrooms are edible. Some only once and for all.

Be nice to your kids.
They are the ones who will choose your retirement home.

Friends come and go.
Enemies add up.

If love is blind, use your hand.

If Woman were good, God would have a wife.
If she were trustworthy, Satan would not wear horns.[62]

Some men love their wives so much that, not to use them,
they use other men's wives.

If sometimes you feel depressed, remember:
one day you were the quickest sperm of all.

Bosses are like clouds,
when they disappear the atmosphere is much nicer.

Hierarchy is like a shelf: the higher, the more useless.

Your future depends on your dreams.
Don't waste time, go to bed now.

Love is like the flu.
You catch it in the street and cure it in bed.

Men would lie less if women asked less questions.

Marriage Quotes

"In my house I'm the boss, my wife is just the decision maker."
(*Woody Allen*)

"My wife and I were happy for twenty years. Then we met."
(*Rodney Dangerfield*)

"Ah, yes, divorce. . . from the Latin word meaning to rip out a
man's genitals through his wallet."
(*Robin Williams*)

"A married man should forget his mistakes;
no use two people remembering the same thing."
(*Duane Dewel*)

"When you see a married couple walking down the street,
the one that's a few steps ahead is the one that's mad."
(*Helen Rowland*)

"I have never really understood this liking for war.
It panders to instincts already well catered for in any
respectable domestic establishment."
(*Alan Bennett*)

"Eighty percent of married men cheat in America.
The rest cheat in Europe."
(*Jackie Mason*)

"Marriage is like putting your hand into a bag of snakes in the
hope of pulling out an eel."
(*Leonardo Da Vinci*)

"I don't think I'll get married again.
I'll just find a woman I don't like and give her a house."
(*Lewis Grizzard*)

"I'm the only man in the world with a marriage license made
out to whom it may concern."
(*Mickey Rooney*)

"The difference between divorce and legal separation is that
legal separation gives a husband time to hide his money."
(*Johnny Carson*)

When Insults Had Class

"He has all the virtues I dislike and none of the vices I admire."
(*Winston Churchill*)

"A modest little person, with much to be modest about."
(*Winston Churchill*)

"I have never killed a man,
but I have read many obituaries with great pleasure."
(*Clarence Darrow*)

"He has never been known to use a word that might send a
reader to the dictionary."
(*William Faulkner about Ernest Hemingway*)

"Poor Faulkner. Does he really think big emotions come from
big words?"
(*Ernest Hemingway about William Faulkner*)

"Thank you for sending me a copy of your book;
I'll waste no time reading it."
(*Moses Hadas*)

"He can compress the most words into the smallest idea
of any man I know."
(*Abraham Lincoln*)

"I've had a perfectly wonderful evening. But this wasn't it."
(*Groucho Marx*)

"I didn't attend the funeral, but I sent a nice letter saying
I approved of it."
(*Mark Twain*)

"He has no enemies, but is intensely disliked by his friends."
(*Oscar Wilde*)

"I am enclosing two tickets to the first night of my new play;
bring a friend… if you have one."
(*George Bernard Shaw to Winston Churchill*)

"Cannot possibly attend first night, will attend second. . .
if there is one."
(*Winston Churchill, in response*)

"I feel so miserable without you; it's almost like having you here."
(*Stephen Bishop*)

"He is a self-made man and worships his creator."
(*John Bright*)

"I've just learned about his illness. Let's hope it's nothing trivial."
(*Irvin S. Cobb*)

"He is not only dull himself; he is the cause of dullness in others."
(*Samuel Johnson*)

"He is simply a shiver looking for a spine to run up."
(*Paul Keating*)

"He had delusions of adequacy."
(*Walter Kerr*)

"There's nothing wrong with you that reincarnation won't cure."
(*Jack E. Leonard*)

"He has the attention span of a lightning bolt."
(*Robert Redford*)

"They never open their mouths without subtracting from the
sum of human knowledge."
(*Thomas Brackett Reed*)

"He inherited some good instincts from his Quaker forebears,
but by diligent hard work, he overcame them."
(*James Reston about Richard Nixon*)

"In order to avoid being called a flirt, she always yielded easily."
(*Charles, Count Talleyrand*)

"He loves nature in spite of what it did to him."
(*Forrest Tucker*)

"Why do you sit there looking like an envelope without any
address on it?"
(*Mark Twain*)

"His mother should have thrown him away and kept the stork."
(*Mae West*)

"Some cause happiness wherever they go; others, whenever they go."
(*Oscar Wilde*)

"He uses statistics as a drunken man uses lamp-posts... for support rather than illumination."
(*Andrew Lang, 1844-1912*)

"He has Van Gogh's ear for music."
(*Billy Wilder*)

'So-True' Quotes

"Put your hand on a hot stove for a minute, and it seems like an hour. Sit with a pretty girl for an hour, and it seems like a minute. THAT'S relativity."
(*Albert Einstein*)

"The brain is a wonderful organ. It starts working the moment you get up in the morning and does not stop until you get into the office."
(*Robert Frost*)

"The trouble with being punctual is that nobody's there to appreciate it."
(*Franklin P. Jones*)

"We must believe in luck. For how else can we explain the
success of those we don't like?"
(*Jean Cocturan*)

"It matters not whether you win or lose;
what matters is whether I win or lose.
(*Darrin Weinberg*)

"Help a man when he is in trouble and he will remember you
when he is in trouble again."
(*Unknown*)

"Complex problems have simple, easy to understand
wrong answers."
(*Unknown*)

"It is not exactly cheating, I prefer to consider it creative
problem solving."
(*Unknown*)

"Whoever said money can't buy happiness didn't
know where to shop."
(*Unknown*)

"Alcohol doesn't solve any problems, but then again,
neither does milk."
(*Unknown*)

"Forgive your enemies but remember their names."

(Unknown)

"The number of people watching you is directly proportional to the stupidity of your action."

(Unknown)

"Don't worry that the world ends today, it's already tomorrow in Australia!"

(Unknown)

7) POETRY

The National Poetry Contest had come down to two, a Yale graduate and a redneck from Texas. They were given a word, then allowed two minutes to study the word and come up with a poem that contained the word. The word they were given was "Timbuktu." First to recite his poem was the Yale graduate. He stepped to the microphone and said,

"Slowly across the desert sand

Trekked a lonely Caravan;

Men on camels, two by two,

Destination Timbuktu."

The crowd went crazy! No way could the redneck top that, they thought.. . . The Texas redneck calmly made his way to the microphone and recited:

"Me and Tim a huntin' went.

Met three whores in a pop-up tent.

They was three, and we was two,

So I bucked one, and Timbuktu."

Leather

When a woman wears leather clothing,

a man's heart beats quicker,

his throat gets dry,

he goes weak in the knees

and he begins to think irrationally.

Ever wonder why?

Because she smells like a new truck...

Golf

In my hand I hold a ball,

White and dimpled rather small,

Oh, how bland it does appear,

This harmless looking little sphere.

By its size I could not guess

The awesome strength it does possess.

But since I fell beneath its spell

I've wandered through the fires of Hell.

My life has not been quite the same,

Since I choose to play this stupid game.

It rules my mind for hours on end.

A fortune it has made me spend.

It's made me swear and yell and cry,

I hate myself and want to die.

It promises a thing called par,

If I can hit it and far.

To master such a tiny ball

Should not be very hard at all.

But my desires the ball refuses

And does exactly what it chooses.

It hooks and slices dribbles and dies,

And even disappears before my eyes.

Often it will take a whim

To hit a tree or take a swim.

With miles of grass on which to land

It finds a tiny patch of sand.

It has me offering up my soul

If only it would find the hole.

It makes me whimper like a pup

And swear that I will give it up.

And take a drink to ease my sorrow

But it knows that I'll be back tomorrow.

Black and White

Dear White Brother,

When I was born, I was black,

When I grew up, I was black,

When I'm in the sunshine, I am black,

When I am sick, I am black,

When I die, I'll be black.

While you, White Man,

When you were born, you were pink,

When you grew up, you were white,

When you are in the sunshine, you are red,

When you are cold, you are blue,

When you are scared, you are green,

When you are sick, you are yellow,

When you die, you'll be grey.

And you dare call me "a colored man"…

Chinese (?) Proverb

With money you can buy a house but not a home.

With money you can buy a clock but not time.

With money you can buy a bed but not sleep.

With money you can buy a book but not knowledge.

With money you can buy a doctor but not good health.

With money you can buy a position but not respect.

With money you can buy blood but not life.

With money you can buy sex but not love.

Poem to a Friend

Around the corner I have a friend,

In this great city that has no end,

Yet the days go by and weeks rush on,

And before I know it, a year is gone.

And I never see my old friends' face,

For life is a swift and terrible race,

He knows I like him just as well,

As in the days when I rang his bell.

And he rang mine but we were younger then,

And now we are busy, tired men.

Tired of playing a foolish game,

Tired of trying to make a name.

"Tomorrow" I say! "I will call on Jim

Just to show that I'm thinking of him."

But tomorrow comes and tomorrow goes,

And distance between us grows and grows.

Around the corner, yet miles away,

"Here's a telegram sir," "Jim died today."

And that's what we get and deserve in the end.

Around the corner, a vanished friend.

Audrey Hepburn's "Beauty Tips"

For attractive lips, speak words of kindness.

For lovely eyes, seek out the good in people.

For a slim figure, share your food with the hungry.

For beautiful hair, let a child run his/her fingers through it once

a day.

For poise, walk with the knowledge that you never walk alone.

People, even more than things, have to be restored,

Renewed, revived, reclaimed, and redeemed;

Never throw out anyone.

Remember, if you ever need a helping hand,

You will find one at the end of each of your arms.

As you grow older, you will discover that you have two hands;

One for helping yourself, and the other for helping others.

8) NATIONALITIES

Islanders

On a chain of beautiful deserted islands in the middle of nowhere, the people listed below were stranded together.

Two Italian men and one Italian woman.

Two Frenchmen and one French woman.

Two German men and one German woman.

Two Greek men and one Greek woman.

Two Englishmen and one English woman.

Two Bulgarian men and one Bulgarian woman.

Two Japanese men and one Japanese woman.

Two Chinese men and one Chinese woman.

Two Irishmen and one Irish woman.

Two American men and one American woman.

One month later, on these absolutely stunning deserted islands in the middle of nowhere, various things occur.

One Italian man kills the other Italian man for the Italian woman.

The two Frenchmen and the French woman are living happily together in a *ménage à trois*.

The two German men have a strict weekly schedule of alternating visits with the German woman.

The two Greek men are sleeping with each other and the Greek woman is cleaning and cooking for them.

The two Englishmen are waiting for someone to introduce them to the English woman.

The two Bulgarian men took one look at the Bulgarian woman and started swimming to another island.

The two Japanese have faxed Tokyo and are awaiting instructions.

The two Chinese men have set up a pharmacy/liquor store/ restaurant/laundry, and have got the Chinese woman pregnant in order to supply employees for their store.

The two Irishmen divided the island into North and South and set up a distillery. They do not remember if sex is in the picture because it gets somewhat foggy after a few liters of coconut whisky. However, they're satisfied because the English aren't having any fun.

The two American men are contemplating suicide, because the American woman complains relentlessly about her body, the true nature of feminism, what the sun is doing to her skin, how she can do anything they can do, the necessity of fulfillment, the equal division of household chores, how sand and palm trees make her look fat, how her last boyfriend respected her opinion and treated her nicer than they do, how her relationship with her mother is the root cause of all her problems, and why didn't they bring a cell phone so they could call 911 and get them all rescued off this God-forsaken deserted island in the middle of freaking nowhere so she can get her nails done and go shopping...

British Hospitality

An American tourist in London decides to skip his tour group and explore the city on his own. He wanders around, seeing the sights, and occasionally stopping at a quaint pub to soak up the local culture, chat with the lads, and have a pint of Guinness®. After a while, he finds himself in a very high class neighborhood. . . big, stately residences. . . no pubs, no stores, no restaurants, and worst of all. . . NO PUBLIC RESTROOMS. He really, really has to go, after all those Guinnesses®. He finds a narrow side street, with high walls surrounding the adjacent buildings and decides to use the wall to solve his problem. As he is unzipping, he is tapped on the shoulder by a London Bobbie, who says, "I say, Sir, you simply cannot do that here, you know." "I'm very sorry, officer," replies the American, "but I really, really HAVE TO GO, and I just can't find a public restroom." "Ah, yes," said the Bobbie, "just follow me." He leads him to a back "delivery alley" then along a wall to a gate, which he opens. "In there," points the Bobbie. "Whiz away, anywhere you want." The fellow enters and finds himself in the most beautiful garden he has ever seen. Manicured grass lawns, statuary, fountains, sculptured hedges, and huge beds of gorgeous flowers, all in perfect bloom. Since he has the cop's blessing, he zips down and unburdens himself and is greatly relieved. As he goes back through the gate, he says to the Bobbie, "That was really decent of you. Is that British Hospitality?" "No," replied the Bobbie, with a satisfied smile on his face, "that is the French Embassy."

English Language

Reasons below why the English language is so hard to learn.

1. The bandage was wound around the wound.
2. The farm was used to produce produce.
3. The dump was so full that it had to refuse more refuse.
4. We must polish the Polish furniture.
5. He could lead if he would get the lead out.
6. The soldier decided to desert his dessert in the desert.
7. Since there is no time like the present, he thought it was time to present the present.
8. A bass was painted on the head of the bass drum.
9. When shot at, the dove dove into the bushes.
10. I did not object to the object.
11. The insurance was invalid for the invalid.
12. There was a row among the oarsmen about how to row.
13. They were too close to the door to close it.
14. The buck does funny things when the does are present.
15. A seamstress and a sewer fell down into a sewer line.
16. To help with planting, the farmer taught his sow to sow.
17. The wind was too strong to wind the sail.
18. After a number of injections my jaw got number.
19. Upon seeing the tear in the painting of the shed I shed a tear.
20. I had to subject the subject to a series of tests.
21. How can I intimate this to my most intimate friend?
22. There is neither egg in eggplant nor ham in hamburger; neither apple nor pine in pineapple.

23.   English muffins weren't invented in England nor French fries in France.

24.   Sweetmeats are candies while sweetbreads, which aren't sweet, are meat.

25.   Quicksand works slowly, boxing rings are square and a guinea pig is neither from Guinea nor is it a pig.

26.   And why is it that writers write but fingers don't fing, grocers don't groce and hammers don't ham?

27.   If the plural of tooth is teeth, why isn't the plural of booth beeth? One goose, two geese. So one moose, two meese?

28.   Doesn't it seem crazy that you can make amends but not one amend.

29.   If you have a bunch of odds and ends and get rid of all but one of them, what do you call it? Is it an odd, or an end?

30.   If teachers taught, why didn't preachers praught? If a vegetarian eats vegetables, what does a humanitarian eat? In what language do people recite at a play and play at a recital?

31.   Ship by truck and send cargo by ship?

32.   Have noses that run and feet that smell?

33.   How can a slim chance and a fat chance be the same, while a wise man and a wise guy are opposites?

34.   You have to marvel at the unique lunacy of a language in which your house can burn up as it burns down, in which you fill in a form by filling it out and in which, an alarm goes off by going on.

35. English was invented by people, not computers, and it reflects the creativity of the human race, which, of course, is not a race at all.

36. That is why, when the stars are out, they are visible, but when the lights are out, they are invisible.

37. George Bernard Shaw wrote a *London Times* article when he was campaigning for spelling reform. He gave the following example: if *gh* is pronounced *f* as in *enough*, if *o* is pronounced *e* as in *women*, if *th* is pronounced *sh* as in *motion*, then the correct way to spell *fish* should be *ghoti*.

The Irish

One fine day in Ireland, a guy is out golfing and gets up to the sixteenth hole. He tees up and cranks one. Unfortunately, it goes into the woods on the side of the fairway. He goes looking for his ball and comes across this little guy with this huge knot on his head and the golf ball lying right beside him. "Goodness," says the golfer, and proceeds to revive the poor little guy. Upon awakening, the little guy says, "Well, you caught me fair and square; I am a leprechaun. I will grant you three wishes." The man says, "I can't take anything from you, I'm just glad I didn't hurt you too badly," and walks away.

Watching the golfer depart, the leprechaun thinks, "Well, he was a nice enough guy and he did catch me so I have to do something for him. I'll give him the three things that I would want – unlimited money, a great golf game, and a great sex life." A year passes and the same golfer is out golfing on the same course at the sixteenth hole. He gets up and hits one into the same woods, goes looking for his ball, and comes across the same leprechaun. He asks the leprechaun how he is and the leprechaun replies, "I'm fine, and might I ask how your golf game is?" The golfer says, "It's great! I hit under par every time." The leprechaun says, "I did that for you. And how is your money holding out?" The golfer says, "Well, now that you mention it, every time I put my hand in my pocket, I pull out a hundred dollar bill." The leprechaun smiles and says, "I did that for you too. And how is your sex life?" The golfer looks at him shyly and says, "Well, maybe once or twice a week." The leprechaun is floored and stammers, "Once or twice a week?!" The golfer, a little embarrassed, looks at him and says, "Well, that's not too bad for a Catholic priest in a small parish."

■

After having their eleventh child, an Irish couple decides that is enough, as they cannot afford a larger bed. So the husband goes to his doctor and tells him that he and his wife don't want to have any more children. The doctor tells him there is a procedure called a vasectomy that would fix the problem but it is expensive. A less costly alternative is to go home, get a firework, light it, put it in a beer can, then hold the can up to his ear and count to ten. The husband says to the doctor, "B'Jayzus, I may not be the smartest guy in the world, but I don't see how putting a firework in a beer can next to my ear is going to help me." "Trust me, it will do the job", says the doctor. So the man goes home, lights a banger and puts it in a beer can. He holds the can up to his ear and begins to count: "One, two, three, four, five…," at which point he pauses, places the beer can between his legs so he can continue counting on his other hand.

Note: According to the (Sydney-based) unknown author, this procedure also works in New Zealand, Tasmania and South Australia.

■

An Irish priest is driving down to New York and gets stopped for speeding in Connecticut. The state trooper smells alcohol on the priest's breath and then sees an empty wine bottle on the floor of the car. He says, "Sir, have you been drinking?" "Just water," says the priest. The trooper says, "Then why do I smell wine?" The priest looks at the bottle and says, "Good Lord! He's done it again!"

■

Drunk Ole Mulvihill (from the Northern Irish Clan) staggers into a Catholic Church, enters a confessional box, sits down but says nothing. The Priest coughs a few times to get his attention but the Ole just sits there. Finally, the Priest pounds three times on the wall. The drunk mumbles, "Ain't no use knockin, there's no paper on this side either."

■

Mary Clancy goes up to Father O'Grady's after his Sunday morning service, and she's in tears. He says, "So what's bothering you, Mary my dear?" She says, "Oh, Father, I've got terrible news. My husband passed away last night." The priest says, "Oh, Mary, that is terrible. Tell me, did he have any last requests?" She says, "That he did, Father." The priest asks, "What did he ask, Mary?" "He said, 'Please Mary, put down that damn gun'!"

■

An Irish daughter has not been home for over five years. Upon her return, her father curses her, "Where have you been all this time, you ingrate! Why didn't you write us, not even a line to let us know how you were doing? Why didn't you call? You little tramp! Don't you know what you put your sweet mother through??!!" The girl, crying, replies, "Sniff, sniff. . . Dad. . . I became a prostitute..." "WHAT!!? Out of here, you shameless harlot! Sinner! You're a disgrace to this family – I don't ever want to see you again!" "OK, Dad but I just came back to give Mom this luxury fur coat, title to a ten bed-room mansion, plus a savings account for a million dollars. For my little brother, this gold Rolex®, and for you Daddy the new Mercedes-Benz® that's parked outside plus a lifetime membership to the Country Club. . . (takes a breath). . . an invitation for you all to spend New Years' Eve on board my new yacht in the Riviera, and...." "Now, what was it you said you had become?" Girl, crying again, "Sniff, sniff. . . A prostitute Dad! . . . Sniff, sniff" "Oh! Saints Preserve Us! – You scared me half to death, girl! I thought you said a Protestant. Come here and give your old man a hug!"

■

Late one Friday night, a policeman spots a man driving very erratically through the streets of Dublin. He pulls the man over and asks him if he has been drinking that evening. "Aye, so I have. It's Friday, you know, so me and the lads stopped by the pub where I had six or seven pints. And then there was something called 'Happy Hour' and they served these mar-gar-itos which are quite good. I had four or five of those. Then I had to drive me friend Mike home and of course I had to go in for a couple of Guinnesses® – couldn't be rude, ye know. Then I stopped on the way home to get another bottle for later." Then, the man fumbles around in his coat until he locates his bottle of whiskey, which he holds up for inspection. The officer sighs, and says, "Sir, I'm afraid I'll need you to step out of the car and take a breathalyzer test." Indignantly, the man says, "Why? Don't ye believe me?!"

■

Paddy is driving down the street in a sweat because he has an important meeting and can't find a parking place. Looking up to heaven he says, "Lord take pity on me. If you find me a parking place I will go to Mass every Sunday for the rest of me life and give up me Irish whiskey!" Miraculously, a parking place appears. Paddy looks up again and says, "Never mind, I found one."

■

Father Murphy walks into a pub in Donegal, and says to the first man he meets, "Do you want to go to Heaven?" The man says, "I do, Father." The priest says, "Then stand over there against the wall." Then the priest asks the second man, "Do you want to go to Heaven?" "Certainly, Father," is the man's reply. "Then stand over there against the wall," says the priest. Then Father Murphy walks up to O'Toole and says, "Do you want to go to Heaven?" O'Toole says, "No, I don't Father." The priest says, "I don't believe this. You mean to tell me that when you die you don't want to go to Heaven?" O'Toole says, "Oh, when I die, yes. I thought you were getting a group together to go right now."

■

Patrick is in New York. He is patiently waiting and watching the traffic cop on a busy street crossing. The cop stop the flow of traffic and shout, "Okay, pedestrians." Then he allows the traffic to pass. He does this several times, and Paddy still stands on the sidewalk. After the cop has shouted, "Pedestrians!" for the tenth time, Patrick goes over to him and says, "Is it not about time ye let the Catholics across?"

■

Gallagher opens the morning newspaper and is dumbfounded to read in the obituary column that he has died. He quickly phones his best friend, Finney. "Did you see the paper?" asked Gallagher. "They say I died!!" "Yes, I saw it!" replies Finney. "Where are ye callin' from?"

■

Walking into the bar, Mike says to Charlie the bartender, "Pour me a stiff one – just had another fight with the little woman." "Oh yeah?" says Charlie, "And how did this one end?" "When it was over," Mike replies, "she came to me on her hands and knees." "Really?" says Charles, "now that's a switch! What did she say?" "She said, 'Come out from under the bed, you little chicken'."

■

A doctor wants to get off work and play golf, so he approaches his Irish assistant Paddy: "I am going golfing tomorrow Paddy and I don't want to close the clinic. I want you to take care of the clinic and take care of all of our patients." "Yes, sir!" answers Paddy. The doctor goes off to golf and returns the following day and asks, "So, Paddy, how was your day?" Paddy tells him that he took care of three patients. "The first one had a headache so I gave him Panadol®." "Bravo, mate, and the second one?" asks the doctor. "The second one had stomach burning and I gave him Aspirin." "Excellent. You're good at this and what about the third one?" asks the doctor. "Well, I was sitting here and suddenly the door opens and a woman enters. Like a woman possessed, she undresses herself, taking off everything including her bra and her panties and lies down on the table, and shouts: 'HELP ME! For five years I haven't seen a man!'" "Good God," says the doctor. "What did you do?" "I put drops in her eyes!"

■

Muldoon lived alone in the Irish countryside with only a pet dog for company. One day the dog dies, and Muldoon goes to the parish priest and asks, "Father, my dog is dead. Could ya' be saying' a mass for the poor creature?" Father Patrick replies, "I'm afraid not; we cannot have services for an animal in the church. But there are some Baptists down the lane, and there's no tellin' what they believe. Maybe they'll do something for the creature." Muldoon says, "I'll go right away Father. Do ya' think five grand is enough to donate to them for the service?" Father Patrick exclaims, "Sweet Mary, Mother of Jesus! Why didn't ya tell me the dog was Catholic?"

■

A married Irishman goes into the confessional and says to his priest, "I almost had an affair with another woman." The priest says, "What do you mean, almost?" The Irishman says, "Well, we got undressed and rubbed together, but then I stopped." The priest says, "Rubbing together is the same as putting it in. You're not to see that woman again. For your penance, say five Hail Mary's and put money in the poor box." The Irishman leaves the confessional, says his prayers, and then walks over to the poor box. He pauses for a moment and then starts to leave. The priest, who was watching, quickly runs over to him saying, "I saw that. You didn't put any money in the poor box!" The Irishman replies, "Yeah, but I rubbed it on the box, and according to you, that's the same as putting it in!"

■

A religious young woman goes to confession. Upon entering the confessional, she says, "Forgive me, Father, for I have sinned." The priest says, "Confess your sins and be forgiven." The young woman says, "Last night my boyfriend made mad, passionate love to me seven times." The priest thinks long and hard and then says, "Squeeze seven lemons into a glass and then drink the juice." The young woman asks, "Will this cleanse me of my sins?" The priest says, "No, but it will wipe that smile off of your face."

■

An elderly man walks into a confessional. The following conversation ensues. Man: "I am ninety-two years old, have a wonderful wife of seventy years, many children, grandchildren, and great grandchildren. Yesterday, I picked up two college girls, hitchhiking. We went to a motel, where I had sex with each of them three times." Priest: "Are you sorry for your sins?" Man: "What sins?" Priest: "What kind of a Catholic are you?" Man: "I'm Jewish." Priest: "Why are you telling me all this" Man: "I'm ninety-two years old.. . . I'm telling everybody!"

■

Two men are sitting next to each other at a bar. After a while, one guy looks at the other and says, "I can't help but think, from listening to you, that you're from Ireland." The other guy responds proudly, "Yes, that I am!" The first guy says, "So am I! And where about from Ireland might you be?" The other guy answers, "I'm from Dublin, I am." The first guy responds, "So am I! 'Sure and begorra. And what street did you live on in Dublin?" The other guy says, "A lovely little area it was. I lived on McCleary Street in the old central part of town." The first guy says, "Faith and it's a small world. So did I! So did I! And to what school would you have been going?" The other guy answers, "Well now, I went to St. Mary's, of course." The first guy gets really excited and says, "And so did I. Tell me, what year did you graduate?" The other guy answers, "Well, now, let's see. I graduated in 1964." The first guy exclaims, "The Good Lord must be smiling down upon us! I can hardly believe our good luck at winding up in the same bar tonight. Can you believe it, I graduated from St. Mary's in 1964 my own self!" About this time, Vicky walks into the bar, sits down and orders a beer. Brian, the bartender, walks over to Vicky, shaking his head and mutters, "It's going to be a long night tonight." Vicky asks, "Why do you say that, Brian?" "The Murphy twins are drunk again."

■

One day an Irishman, who has been stranded on a deserted island for more than ten years, sees a speck on the horizon. He thinks to himself, "It's certainly not a ship." As the speck gets closer and closer, he begins to rule out the possibilities of a small boat and even a raft. Suddenly there emerges from the surf a wet-suited black clad figure. Putting aside the scuba gear and the top of the wet suit, there stands a drop-dead gorgeous blonde! The glamorous blonde goes up to the stunned Irishman and says to him, "How long has it been since you had a good cigar?" "Ten years," replies the amazed Irishman. With that, she reaches over and unzipps a waterproof pocket on the left sleeve of her wetsuit and pulls out a fresh package of cigars. He takes one, lights it, and takes a long drag. "Faith and b'gorrah," says the man, "that is so good I'd almost forgotten how great a smoke can be!" "And how long has it been since you've had a drop of good Powers® Irish Whiskey?" asks the blonde. Trembling, the castaway replies, "Ten years." Hearing that, the blonde reaches over to her right sleeve, unzips a pocket, removes a flask and hands it to him. He opens the flask and took a long drink. "Tis the nectar of the gods! States the Irishman – truly fantastic." At this point the gorgeous blonde starts to slowly unzip the long front of her wet suit, right down the middle. She looks at the trembling man and asks, "And how long has it been since you played around?" With tears in his eyes, the Irishman fell to his knees and sobbed – "Jesus, Mary and Joseph! Don't tell me you've got golf clubs in there too!"

Polish Eye Test

A Polish immigrant goes to the Roads Authority to apply for a driver's license. He has to take an eye sight test. The lady at the counter asks, "Can you read this?"

C Z W I X N O S T A C Z

"Read it?" the Polish man replies, "I know the guy."

Cows and International Systems

1. SOCIALISM: You have two cows and you give one to your neighbor.
2. COMMUNISM: You have two cows. The Government takes both and gives you some milk.
3. FASCISM: You have two cows. The Government takes both and sells you some milk.
4. NAZISM: You have two cows. The Government takes both and shoots you.
5. BUREAUCRATISM: You have two cows. The Government takes both, shoots one, milks the other and throws the milk away.
6. SURREALISM: You have two giraffes. The government requires you to take harmonica lessons.

7. TRADITIONAL CAPITALISM: You have two cows. You sell one and buy a bull. Your herd multiplies, and the economy grows. You sell them and retire on the income.

8. AN AMERICAN CORPORATION: You have two cows. You sell one, and force the other to produce the milk of four cows. Later, you hire a consultant to analyze why the cow dropped dead.

9. ENRON VENTURE CAPITALISM: You have two cows. You sell three of them to your publicly listed company, using letters of credit opened by your brother-in-law at the bank, then execute a debt/equity swap with an associated general offer so that you get all four cows back, with a tax exemption for five cows. The milk rights of the six cows are transferred via an intermediary to a Cayman Island Company secretly owned by the majority shareholder who sells the rights to all seven cows back to your listed company. The annual report says the company owns eight cows, with an option on one more. You sell one cow to buy a new president of the United States, leaving you with nine cows. No balance sheet provided with the release. The public then buys your bull.

10. THE ANDERSEN[63] MODEL: You have two cows. You shred them.

11. A FRENCH CORPORATION: You have two cows. You go on strike because you want three cows.

12. A JAPANESE CORPORATION: You have two cows. You redesign them so they are one-tenth the size of an ordi-

nary cow and produce twenty times the milk. You then create a clever cow cartoon image called "Cowkimon" and market them world-wide.

13.   A GERMAN CORPORATION: You have two cows. You re-engineer them so they live for a hundred years, eat once a month, and milk themselves.

14.   A BRITISH CORPORATION: You have two cows. Both are mad.

15.   AN ITALIAN CORPORATION: You have two cows, but you don't know where they are. You break for lunch.

16.   A RUSSIAN CORPORATION: You have two cows. You count them and learn you have five cows. You count them again and learn you have forty-two cows. You count them again and learn you have two cows. You stop counting cows and open another bottle of vodka.

17.   A SWISS CORPORATION: You have three thousand cows, none of which belong to you. You charge the owners for storing them.

18.   A CHINESE CORPORATION: You have two cows. You have three hundred people milking them. You claim full employment, high bovine productivity, and arrest the newsman who reported the numbers.

19.   A HONG KONG CORPORATION: You have two cows on the eighteenth Floor. You have a Filipino maid to milk them. The cows get SARS and you blame it on Tung Chee Wah.[64]

20.   AN ARKANSAS CORPORATION: You have two cows. That one on the left is kinda cute. . .

21.   AN INDIAN CORPORATION: You have two cows. You worship them.

22.   AN IRAQI CORPORATION: Everyone thinks you have lots of cows. You tell them that you have none. No one believes you, so they bomb you and invade your country. You still have no cows, but at least now you are part of a Democracy. . .

23.   AN AUSTRALIAN CORPORATION: You have two cows. Business seems pretty good. You close the office and go for a few beers.

24.   AN IRISH CORPORATION. You have two cows. . . or is it three? What matters? Aren't you well off to have even one?

Canadian Fishing

A redneck is stopped by a game warden just outside of North Bay, Ontario (Canada) with two ice chests of fish, leaving an area lake well known for the fishing. The game warden asks the man, "Do you have a license to catch those fish?" "Naw, my friend, I ain't got no license. These are my pet fish." "Pet fish?" "Yep. Every night I take these fish down to the lake and let 'em swim 'round for a while. Then I whistle and they jump right back into this ice chest and I take 'em home." "That's a bunch of hooey! Fish can't do that!" The redneck looks at the game warden for a moment and then says, "It's the truth. I'll show you. It really works." "Okay, I've GOT to see this!" The redneck pours the fish into the river and stands and waits. After several minutes, the game warden turns to him and says, "Well?" "Well, what?" says the redneck. "When are you going to call them back?" "Call who back?" "The FISH!" "What fish?"

Canadian Billion

The next time you hear a politician use the words "billion" casually, think about whether you want that politician spending your tax money. A billion is a difficult number to comprehend, but one Canadian advertising agency did a good job of putting that figure into perspective in one of its releases of 2006:

A billion seconds ago it was 1959.[65]

A billion minutes ago Jesus was alive.[66]

A billion hours ago our ancestors were living in the Stone Age.

A billion dollars ago was only eight hours and twenty minutes, at the rate Ottawa spends it.

Almost French

Did you hear about the guy in Paris who almost got away with stealing several paintings from the Louvre? After planning the crime and getting in and out past security, he was captured only two blocks away when his minivan ran out of gas. When asked how he could mastermind such a crime and then make such an obvious error, he replied, "Monsieur, I had no Monet to buy Degas to make the Van Gogh." And you thought I lacked De Gaulle to tell you a story like this!

Indian English

An Italian, a Frenchman, and an Indian go for a job interview in England. They are told that they must compose a sentence in English with three main words: green, pink, and yellow The Italian is first: "I wake up in the morning. I see the yellow sun. I see the green grass and I hope it will be a pink day." The Frenchman is next: "I wake up in the morning, I eat a yellow banana, a green pepper and in the evening I watch the Pink Panther on TV." Last is the Indian: "I wake up in the morning, I hear the phone, 'green-green', I 'pink' up the phone and I say 'Yellow?'."

9) SIGNS, HEADLINES AND ANNOUNCEMENTS

Golf Club

Here is an actual sign (allegedly) posted at a golf club in Scottsdale, Arizona (U.S.A.):

BACK STRAIGHT, KNEES BENT, FEET SHOULDER WIDTH APART.

FORM A LOOSE GRIP.

KEEP YOUR HEAD DOWN!

AVOID A QUICK BACK SWING.

STAY OUT OF THE WATER

TRY NOT TO HIT ANYONE.

IF YOU ARE TAKING TOO LONG, LET OTHERS GO AHEAD OF YOU.

DON'T STAND DIRECTLY IN FRONT OF OTHERS.

QUIET PLEASE. . . WHILE OTHERS ARE PREPARING TO GO.

DON'T TAKE EXTRA STROKES.

WELL DONE – NOW FLUSH THE URINAL, GO OUTSIDE, AND
TEE OFF.

Actual British Signs

(Authenticity unverified)

Spotted in a toilet of a London office:
TOILET OUT OF ORDER. PLEASE USE FLOOR BELOW.

In a Laundromat:
AUTOMATIC WASHING MACHINES: PLEASE REMOVE ALL
YOUR CLOTHES WHEN THE LIGHT GOES OUT.

In a London department store:
BARGAIN BASEMENT UPSTAIRS.

In an office:
WOULD THE PERSON WHO TOOK THE STEP LADDER
YESTERDAY PLEASE BRING IT BACK OR FURTHER STEPS
WILL BE TAKEN.

In an office:
AFTER TEA BREAK STAFF SHOULD EMPTY THE TEAPOT
AND STAND UPSIDE DOWN ON THE DRAINING BOARD.

Outside a second-hand shop:
WE EXCHANGE ANYTHING – BICYCLES, WASHING
MACHINES, ETC. WHY NOT BRING YOUR WIFE ALONG AND
GET A WONDERFUL BARGAIN?

Notice in health food shop window:
CLOSED DUE TO ILLNESS.

Spotted in a safari park:
ELEPHANTS PLEASE STAY IN YOUR CAR.

Seen during a conference:
FOR ANYONE WHO HAS CHILDREN AND DOESN'T KNOW
IT, THERE IS A DAY CARE ON THE FIRST FLOOR.

Notice in a field:
THE FARMER ALLOWS WALKERS TO CROSS THE FIELD
FOR FREE, BUT THE BULL CHARGES.

Message on a leaflet:
IF YOU CANNOT READ, THIS LEAFLET WILL TELL YOU
HOW TO GET LESSONS.

On a repair shop door:
WE CAN REPAIR ANYTHING. (PLEASE KNOCK HARD ON
THE DOOR – THE BELL DOESN'T WORK).

Various Signs

At an unidentified zoo:
PLEASE BE SAFE: DO NOT STAND, SIT, CLIMB OR LEAN ON
ZOO FENCES. IF YOU FALL, ANIMALS CAN EAT YOU AND
THAT MIGHT MAKE THEM SICK. THANK YOU.

In a Dublin bus:
NOTICE TO NITELINK® PASSENGERS:
LADIES, THE POLES ARE FITTED FOR YOUR SAFETY.
NO DANCING.

In front of St. Cyril of Alexandria Church (Galveston, Texas):
STAYING IN BED SHOUTING OH GOD! DOES NOT
CONSTITUTE GOING TO CHURCH.

In an unidentified factory:
CAUTION: THIS MACHINE HAS NO BRAIN. USE YOUR OWN.

In a North Vancouver (Canada) Natural Park:
ATTENTION DOG GUARDIANS: PICK UP AFTER YOUR DOG.
THANK YOU. ATTENTION DOGS: GRRR, BARK, WOOF.
GOOD DOG.

In an unidentified public restroom:
OUR AIM IS TO KEEP THIS BATHROOM CLEAN.
GENTLEMEN: YOUR AIM WILL HELP. STAND CLOSER.
IT'S SHORTER THAN WHAT YOU THINK.
LADIES: PLEASE REMAIN SEATED FOR THE WHOLE
PERFORMANCE.

In an unidentified bar or restaurant:
PLEASE DON'T THROW YOUR CIGARETTES ON THE
FLOOR. COCKROACHES ARE GETTING CANCER.

On the window of a leather goods shop in Edinburgh, U.K.:
MR TOSKANA HAS HAD AN EXPENSIVE DIVORCE AND
NOW NEEDS THE MONEY. SO SALE NOW ON!

News Headlines

(Allegedly found in U.S. newspapers in 2003 –
Authenticity unverified)
Crack Found on Governor's Daughter.
Something Went Wrong in the Jet Crash, Expert Says
Police Begin Campaign to Run Down Jaywalkers
Iraqi Head Seeks Arms
Is There a Ring of Debris around Uranus?
Prostitutes Appeal to Pope
Panda Mating Fails; Veterinarian Takes Over

Actual American Bumper Stickers

(Authenticity Unverified)
Everyone has a photographic memory
....some just don't have any film.

Your ridiculous little opinion has been noted.

I used to have a handle on life. . . but it broke off.

WANTED: Meaningful Overnight Relationship.

Some people just don't know how to drive...
I call these people "Everybody But Me."

Heart Attacks...God's revenge for eating His animal friends.

Don't like my driving? Then quit watching me.

If you can read this. . . I can slam on my brakes and sue you.

Some people are only alive because it is illegal to shoot them.

Try not to let your mind wander, it is too small
and fragile to be out by itself.

Hang up and drive!!

Jesus loves you. . . but everyone else thinks you are an ass.

Impotence. . . Nature's way of saying "No hard feelings."

Welcome to Canada:
....now speak English.

Airline Announcements

*(Authenticity Unverified by the Author
Except for the Last One)*

All too rarely, airline attendants make an effort to make the in flight "safety lecture" and announcements a bit more entertaining. Here are some real examples that have been heard or reported.

1. On a Southwest flight (SW has no assigned seating, you just sit where you want), passengers are apparently having a hard time choosing, when a flight attendant announces, *"People, people we're not picking out furniture here, find a seat and get in it!"*

2. On a Continental Flight with a very "senior" flight attendant crew, the pilot says, *"Ladies and gentlemen, we've reached cruising altitude and will be turning down the cabin lights. This is for your comfort and to enhance the appearance of your flight attendants."*

3. On landing, the stewardess says, *"Please be sure to take all of your belongings. If you're going to leave anything, please make sure it's something we'd like to have."*

4. *"There may be fifty ways to leave your lover but there are only four ways out of this airplane."*

5. *"Thank you for flying Delta Business Express. We hope you enjoyed giving us the business as much as we enjoyed taking you for a ride."*

6. After a particularly rough landing during thunderstorms in Memphis, a flight attendant on a Northwest flight announces, *"Please take care when opening the overhead compartments because, after a landing like that, sure as hell everything has shifted."*

7. From a Southwest Airlines employee: *"Welcome aboard Southwest Flight 245 to Tampa. To operate your seat belt, insert the metal tab into the buckle, and pull tight. It works just like every other seat belt; and, if you don't*

know how to operate one, you probably shouldn't be out in public unsupervised."

8. *"In the event of a sudden loss of cabin pressure, masks will descend from the ceiling. Stop screaming, grab the mask, and pull it over your face. If you have a small child with you, secure your mask before assisting with theirs. If you are with more than one small child, pick your favorite."*

9. *"Weather at our destination is fifty degrees Fareinheit with some broken clouds, but we'll try to have them fixed before we arrive. Thank you, and remember, nobody loves you, or your money, more than Southwest Airlines."*

10. *"Your seat cushions can be used for flotation; and, in the event of an emergency water landing, please paddle to shore and take them with our compliments."*

11. *"As you exit the plane, make sure to gather all of your belongings. Anything left behind will be distributed evenly among the flight attendants. Please do not leave children or spouses."*

12. And from the pilot during his welcome message: *"Delta Airlines is pleased to have some of the best flight attendants in the industry. Unfortunately, none of them are on this flight!"*

13. Heard on Southwest Airlines just after a very hard landing in Salt Lake City. The flight attendant comes on the intercom and says, *"That was quite a bump, and I*

know what y'all are thinking. I'm here to tell you it wasn't the airline's fault, it wasn't the pilot's fault, it wasn't the flight attendant's fault, it was the asphalt."

14.   Overheard on an American Airlines flight into Amarillo, Texas, on a particularly windy and bumpy day. During the final approach, the Captain is really having to fight it. After an extremely hard landing, the Flight Attendant says, *"Ladies and Gentlemen, welcome to Amarillo. Please remain in your seats with your seat belts fastened while the Captain taxis what's left of our airplane to the gate!"*

15.   Another flight attendant's comment on a less than perfect landing: *"We ask you to please remain seated as Captain Kangaroo bounces us to the terminal."*

16.   An airline pilot has hammered his ship into the runway really hard. The airline has a policy which requires the first officer to stand at the door while the passengers exit, smile, and give them a *"Thanks for flying our airline."* In light of his bad landing, he has a hard time looking the passengers in the eye, thinking that someone would have a smart comment. Finally everyone has gotten off except for a little old lady walking with a cane. She says, *"Sir; do you mind if I ask you a question?"* *"Why, no, Ma'am,"* replies the pilot. *"What is it?"* The little old lady asks, *"Did we land, or were we shot down?"*

17.   After a real crusher of a landing in Phoenix, the attendant comes on with, *"Ladies and Gentlemen,*

please remain in your seats until Capt. Crash and the Crew have brought the aircraft to a screeching halt against the gate. And, once the tire smoke has cleared and the warning bells are silenced, we'll open the door and you can pick your way through the wreckage to the terminal."

18.   Part of a flight attendant's arrival announcement: *"We'd like to thank you folks for flying with us today. And, the next time you get the insane urge to go blasting through the skies in a pressurized metal tube, we hope you'll think of U.S. Airways."*

19.   Heard on a Southwest Airline flight: *"Ladies and gentlemen, if you wish to smoke, the smoking section on this airplane is on the wing, and if you can light 'em, you can smoke 'em."*

20.   A plane is taking off from John F. Kennedy Airport. After it reaches a comfortable cruising altitude, the captain makes an announcement over the intercom, *"Ladies and gentlemen, this is your captain speaking. Welcome to Flight 293 from New York to Los Angeles. The weather ahead is good and, therefore, we should have a smooth and uneventful flight. Now sit back and relax . . . OH, MY GOD!"* Silence follows, and after a few minutes, the captain comes back on the intercom and says, *"Ladies and Gentlemen, I am so sorry if I scared you earlier. While I was talking to you, the flight attendant accidentally spilled a cup of hot coffee in my lap. You*

should see the front of my pants!" A passenger in Coach yells, *"That's nothing. You should see the back of mine!"*

21.   Finally, one of the announcements by a flight attendant witnessed by the author of this book on a Belgian airline flying from Brussels to Geneva in December 2005: *"During the take-off procedure, the pilot will dim the lights. You may turn on your reading light. However we advise you not to if you wish to steal from your neighbor's pocket."*

Exchanges between Airline Pilots and Control Towers

(Authenticity unverified)

Here are some conversations that the airline passengers don't hear. The following are accounts of actual exchanges between airline pilots and control towers around the world.

Tower: "Delta 351, you have traffic at 10 o'clock, 6 miles!" Delta 351: "Give us another hint, we have digital watches!"

"TWA 2341, for noise abatement turn right 45 degrees." "Center, we are at thirty-five thousand feet. How much noise can we make up here?" "Sir, have you ever heard the noise a 747 makes when it hits a 727?"

From an unknown aircraft waiting in a very long takeoff line: "I'm f...ing bored!" Ground Traffic Control: "Last aircraft transmitting, identify yourself immediately!" Unknown aircraft: "I said I was f. . . ing bored, not f. . . ing stupid!"

Chicago O'Hare Approach Control to a 747: "United 329 heavy, your traffic is a Fokker, one o'clock, three miles, Eastbound." United 239: "Approach, I've always wanted to say this. . . I've got the little Fokker in sight."

A student became lost during a solo cross-country flight. While attempting to locate the aircraft on radar, Air Trafic Control asked, "What was your last known position?" Student: "When I was number one for takeoff."

A DC-10 had come in a little hot and thus had an exceedingly long roll out after touching down. San Jose Tower noted, "American 751, make a hard right turn at the end of the runway, if you are able. If you are not able, take the Guadalupe exit off Highway 101, make a right at the lights and return to the airport."

A military pilot called for a priority landing because his single-engine jet fighter was running "a bit peaked." Air Traffic Control told the fighter jock that he was number two, behind a B-52 that had one engine shut down. "Ah," the fighter pilot remarked, "the dreaded seven-engine approach."

Taxiing down the tarmac, a DC-10 abruptly stopped, turned around and returned to the gate. After an hour-long wait, it finally took off. A concerned passenger asked the flight attendant, "What, exactly, was the problem?" "The pilot was bothered by a noise he heard in the engine," explained the flight attendant. "It took us a while to find a new pilot."

A Pan Am 727 flight waiting for start clearance in Munich overheard the following: Lufthansa (in German): "Ground, what is our start clearance time?" Ground (in English): "If you want an answer you must speak in English." Lufthansa (in English): "I am a German, flying a German airplane, in Germany. Why must I speak English?" Unknown voice from another plane (in a beautiful British accent): "Because you lost the bloody war."

Tower: "Eastern 702, cleared for takeoff, contact Departure on frequency 124.7." Eastern 702: "Tower, Eastern 702 switching to Departure. By the way, after we lifted off we saw some kind of dead animal on the far end of the runway." Tower: "Continental 635, cleared for takeoff behind Eastern 702, contact Departure on frequency 124.7. Did you copy that report from Eastern 702?" Continental 635: "Continental 635, cleared for takeoff, roger; and yes, we copied Eastern. . . we've already notified our caterers."

One day the pilot of a Cherokee 180 was told by the tower to hold short of the active runway while a DC-8 landed. The DC-8 landed, rolled out, turned around, and taxied back past the Cherokee. Some quick-witted comedian in the DC-8 crew got on the radio and said, "What a cute little plane. Did you make it all by yourself?" The Cherokee pilot, not about to let the insult go by, came back with a real zinger: "I made it out of DC-8 parts. Another landing like yours and I'll have enough parts for another one."

The German air controllers at Frankfurt Airport are re-nowned as a short-tempered lot. They not only expect one to know one's gate parking location, but how to get there without any assistance from them. So it was with some amusement that a Pan Am 747 listened to the following exchange between Frankfurt ground control and a British Airways 747, call sign Speedbird 206. Speedbird 206: "Frankfurt, Speedbird 206 clear of active runway." Ground: "Speedbird 206. Taxi to gate Alpha One-Seven." The BA 747 pulled onto the main taxiway and slowed to a stop. Ground: "Speedbird, do you not know where you are going?" Speedbird 206: "Stand by, Ground, I'm looking up our gate location now." Ground (with quite arrogant impatience): "Speedbird 206, have you not been to Frankfurt before?" Speedbird 206 (coolly): "Yes, twice in 1944, but it was dark, — and I didn't land."

While taxiing at London's Gatwick Airport, the crew of a U.S. Air flight departing for Ft. Lauderdale, Florida, made a wrong turn and came nose to nose with a United 727. An irate female ground controller lashed out at the U.S. Air crew, screaming, "U.S. Air 2771, where the hell are you going?! I told you to turn right onto Charlie taxiway! You turned right on Delta! Stop right there. I know it's difficult for you to tell the difference between C and D, but get it right!" Continuing her rage to the embarrassed crew, she was now shouting hysterically, "God! Now you've screwed everything up! It'll take forever to sort this out! You stay right there and don't move till I tell you to! You can expect progressive taxi instructions in about half an hour and I want you to go exactly where I tell you, when I tell you, and how I tell you!

You got that, U.S. Air 2771?" "Yes, ma'am," the humbled crew responded.   Naturally, the ground control communications frequency fell terribly silent after the verbal bashing of U.S. Air 2771.   Nobody wanted to chance engaging the irate ground controller in her current state of mind.   Tension in every cockpit out around Gatwick was definitely running high.   Just then an unknown pilot broke the silence and keyed his microphone, asking, "Wasn't I married to you once?"

Qantas Repair Logs

(Allegedly Genuine – Authenticity Unverified)

After every flight, Australian airline Qantas pilots fill out a form, called a "gripe sheet", which tells mechanics about problems with the aircraft.   The mechanics correct the problems, document their repairs on the form, then the pilots review the gripe sheets right before the next flight.   Never let it be said that ground crews lack a sense of humor.   Here are some of the actual maintenance complaints submitted by the Qantas' pilots (as marked with a P) and the solutions recorded (as marked with an S) by the maintenance engineers.   By the way, it is relevant to note that Qantas is the only major airline in the world that has never, ever, had an accident!

P: Left inside main tire almost needs replacement.
S: Almost replaced left inside main tire.

P: Test flight OK, except auto-land very rough.
S: Auto-land not installed on this aircraft.

P: Something loose in the cockpit.

S: Something tightened in the cockpit.

P: Dead bugs on windshield.

S: Live bugs on backorder.

P: Autopilot in altitude-hold mode produces a 200-feet per minute descent.

S: Cannot reproduce problem on ground.

P: Evidence of a leak on the right main landing gear.

S: Evidence removed.

P: DME[67] volume unbelievably loud.

S: DME volume reset to a more believable level.

P: Friction locks cause throttle levers to stick.

S: That's what friction locks are for.

P: IFF[68] inoperative in OFF mode.

S: IFF always inoperative in OFF mode.

P: Suspected crack in windshield.

S: Suspect you're right.

P: The number 3 engine is missing.

S: Engine found on right wing after a brief search.

P: Aircraft handles funny.

S: Aircraft warned to straighten up, fly right and be serious.

P: Target radar hums.

S: Reprogrammed target radar with lyrics.

P: Mouse in cockpit.

S: Cat installed.

P: Noise coming from under the instrument panel. Sounds like a midget pounding on something with a hammer.

S: Took hammer away from the midget.

LONDON UNDERGROUND ANNOUNCEMENTS

(Authenticity Unverified, but Likelihood High)

A sampling follows of actual announcements that London Tube train drivers have made to their passengers.

"Ladies and Gentlemen, I do apologize for the delay to your service. I know you're all dying to get home, unless, of course, you happen to be married to my ex-wife, in which case you'll want to cross over to the Westbound and go in the opposite direction. Your delay this evening is caused by the line controller suffering from elbow and backside syndrome, not knowing his elbow from his backside. I'll let you know any further information as soon as I'm given any."

■

"Do you want the good news first or the bad news? The good news is that last Friday was my birthday and I hit the town and had a great time . The bad news is that there is a points failure somewhere between Stratford and East Ham, which means we probably won't reach our destination."

■

"Ladies and gentlemen, we apologize for the delay, but there is a security alert at Victoria station and we are therefore stuck here for the foreseeable future, so let's take our minds off it and pass some time together. All together now… 'Ten green bottles, hanging on a wall'…"

■

"We are now traveling through Baker Street, and as you can see Baker Street is closed. It would have been nice if they had actually told me, so I could tell you earlier, but no, they don't think about things like that."

■

"Beggars are operating on this train, please do NOT encourage these professional beggars, if you have any spare change, please give it to a registered charity. Failing that, give it to me."

■

During an extremely hot rush hour on the Central Line, the driver announced in a West Indian drawl: "Step right this way for the sauna, ladies and gentleman. Unfortunately towels are not provided."

■

"Let the passengers off the train FIRST!" (Pause…) "Oh go on then, stuff yourselves in like sardines, see if I care – I'm going home…."

■

"Please allow the doors to close. Try not to confuse this with 'Please hold the doors open'. The two are distinct and separate instructions."

■

"Please note that the beeping noise coming from the doors means that the doors are about to close. It does not mean throw yourself or your bags into the doors."

■

"To the gentleman wearing the long grey coat trying to get on the second carriage – what part of 'Stand clear of the doors' don't you understand?"

■

"Please move all baggage away from the doors. (Pause.) Please move ALL belongings away from the doors. (Pause.) This is a personal message to the man in the brown suit wearing glasses at the rear of the train – put the pie down, four-eyes, and move your bloody golf clubs away from the door before I come down there and shove them up your ***.

■

"May I remind all passengers that there is strictly no smoking allowed on any part of the Underground. However, if you are smoking a joint, it's only fair that you pass it round the rest of the carriage."

Bathroom Graffiti

(Allegedly Found in U.S. Public Restrooms – Unverified)
Friends don't let friends take home ugly men.
(Women's restroom, Starboard, Dewey Beach, DE)

Beauty is only a light switch away.
(Perkins Library, Duke University, Durham, NC)

If life is a waste of time, and time is a waste of life,
then let's all get wasted together and have the time of our lives.
(Armand's Pizza, Washington, D.C.)

Remember, it's not, "How high are you?" it's "Hi, how are you?"
(Rest stop off Route 81, West Virginia)

Fighting for peace is like screwing for virginity.
The Bayou, Baton Rouge, LO

At the feast of ego everyone leaves hungry.
(Bentley's House of Coffee and Tea, Tucson, AZ)

It's hard to make a comeback when you haven't been
anywhere.
(Written in the dust on the back of a bus, Wickenburg, AZ)

Make love, not war. Hell, do both: GET MARRIED!
(Women's restroom The Filling Station, Bozeman, MT)

If voting could really change things, it would be illegal.
(Restroom of Revolution Books New York, New York)

If pro is opposite of con, then what is the opposite
of progress? Congress!
(Men's restroom House of Representatives, Washington, D.C.)

You're too good for him.

(Sign over mirror in Women's restroom,
Ed Debevic's, Beverly Hills, CA)

No wonder you always go home alone.

(Sign over mirror in Men's restroom,
Ed Debevic's, Beverly Hills, CA)

Actual Answering Machine Answers

(Allegedly Recorded and Verified by the "International
Institute of Answering Machine Answers").[69]

"My wife and I can't come to the phone right now, but if you'll leave your name and number, we'll get back to you as soon as we're finished."

■

"A is for academics, B is for beer. One of those reasons is why we're not here. So leave a message."

■

"Hi. This is John: If you are the phone company, I already sent the money. If you are my parents, please send money. If you are my financial aid institution, you didn't lend me enough money. If you are my friends, you owe me money. If you are a female, don't worry, I have plenty of money."

■

"Hi! Now you say something."

■

"Hi, I'm not home right now but my answering machine is, so you can talk to it instead. Wait for the beep."

■

"Hello. I am David's answering machine. What are you?"

■

(From Japanese friend) "He-lo! This is Sa-to. If you leave
message, I call you soon.
If you leave sexy message, I call sooner!"

■

"Hi! John's answering machine is broken. This is his
refrigerator. Please speak very slowly, and I'll stick your
message to myself with one of these magnets."

■

"Hello, you are talking to a machine. I am capable of
receiving messages. My owners do not need siding,
windows, or a hot tub, and their carpets are clean.
They give to charity through their office and do not
need their picture taken. If you're still with me, leave your
name and number and they will get back to you."

■

"This is not an answering machine; this is a telepathic
thought-recording device. After the tone, think about
your name, your reason for calling and a number where I can
reach you, and I'll think about returning your call."

■

"Hi. I am probably home, I'm just avoiding someone I don't like.
Leave me a message, and if I don't call back, it's you."

■

"Hi, this is George. I'm sorry I can't answer the phone right now. Leave a message, and then wait by your phone until I call you back."

■

"If you are a burglar, then we're probably at home cleaning our weapons right now and can't come to the phone. Otherwise, we probably aren't home and it's safe to leave us a message."

■

"Please leave a message. However, you have the right to remain silent. Everything you say will be recorded and will be used by us."

■

"Hello, you've reached Jim and Sonya. We can't pick up the phone right now, because we're doing something we really enjoy. Sonya likes doing it up and down, and I like doing it left to right. . . real slowly. So leave a message, and when we're done brushing our teeth we'll get back to you."

Australian Tourist Questions and Answers

(Authenticity Unverified)

The questions below about Australia are from potential visitors. They were posted on an Australian Tourism Web site and the answers are the actual responses by the Web site officials, who obviously have some sense of humor.

■

Q: Does it ever get windy in Australia? I have never seen it rain on TV, how do the plants grow? (U.K.).

A: We import all plants fully grown and then just sit around watching them die.

■

Q: Will I be able to see kangaroos in the street? (U.S.A.)

A: Depends how much you've been drinking.

■

Q: I want to walk from Perth to Sydney – can I follow the railroad tracks (Sweden)?

A: Sure, it's only three thousand miles, take lots of water.

■

Q: Are there any ATMs (cash machines) in Australia? Can you send me a list of them in Brisbane, Cairns, Townsville and Hervey Bay? (U.K.)

A: What did your last slave die of?

■

Q: Can you give me some information about hippo racing in Australia? (U.S.A.)

A: A-fri-ca is the big triangle shaped continent south of Europe. Aus-tra-lia is that big island in the middle of the Pacific which does not . . . oh forget it. Sure, the hippo racing is every Tuesday night in Kings Cross. Come naked.

■

Q: Which direction is North in Australia? (U.S.A.)

A: Face south and then turn 180 degrees. Contact us when you get here and we'll send the rest of the directions.

■

Q: Can I bring cutlery into Australia? (U.K.)

A: Why? Just use your fingers like we do.

■

Q: Can you send me the Vienna Boys' Choir schedule? (U.S.A.)

A: Aus-tri-a is that quaint little country bordering Ger-man-y, which is . . . oh forget it. Sure, the Vienna Boys Choir plays every Tuesday night in Kings Cross, straight after the hippo races. Come naked.

■

Q: Can I wear high heels in Australia? (U.K.)

A: You are a British politician, right?

■

Q: Are there supermarkets in Sydney and is milk available all year round? (Germany)

A: No, we are a peaceful civilization of vegan hunter/gatherers. Milk is illegal.

■

Q: Please send a list of all doctors in Australia who can dispense rattlesnake serum. (U.S.A.)

A: Rattlesnakes live in A-meri-ca which is where YOU come from. All Australian snakes are perfectly harmless, can be safely handled and make good pets.

■

Q: I have a question about a famous animal in Australia, but I forget its name. It's a kind of bear and lives in trees. (U.S.A.)

A: It's called a Drop Bear. They are so called because they drop

out of Gum trees and eat the brains of anyone walking under-
neath them. You can scare them off by spraying yourself with
human urine before you go out walking.

■

Q: I have developed a new product that is the fountain of youth.
Can you tell me where I can sell it in Australia? (U.S.A.)
A: Anywhere significant numbers of Americans gather.

■

Q: Can you tell me the regions in Tasmania where the female
population is smaller than the male population? (Italy)
A: Yes, gay night clubs.

■

Q: Do you celebrate Christmas in Australia? (France)
A: Only at Christmas.

■

Q: I was in Australia in 1969 on R+R (Research and Recon-
naissance), and I want to contact the girl I dated while I was
staying in Kings Cross.[70] Can you help? (U.S.A.)
A: Yes, and you will still have to pay her by the hour.

■

Q: Will I be able to speak English most places I go? (U.S.A.)
A: Yes, but you'll have to learn it first.

10) LIFE RULES AND USEFUL ADVICE

Life lessons

Twenty-five things you SHOULD have learned by now.. . .

1.   Your friends love you anyway.

2. Don't worry about what people think – they don't do it very often.

3. Going to church doesn't make you a Christian anymore than standing in a garage makes you a car.

4. Artificial intelligence is no match for natural stupidity.

5. The one thing that unites all human beings, regardless of age, gender, religion, economic status or ethnic background, is that, deep down inside – we ALL believe that we are above average drivers.

6. A person who is nice to you but rude to the waiter is not a nice person.

7. Not one shred of evidence supports the notion that life is serious.

8. There comes a time when you should stop expecting other people to make a big deal about your birthday. That time is age eleven.

9. For every action, there is an equal and opposite government program.

10. If you look like your passport picture, you probably need the trip.

11. Bills travel through the mail at twice the speed of checks.

12. You will never find anybody who can give you a clear and compelling reason why we observe daylight savings time.

13. You should never say anything to a woman that even remotely suggests that you think she's pregnant unless

you can see an actual baby emerging from her at that moment.

14. Men are from Earth. Women are from Earth. Deal with it.

15. No man has ever been shot while doing the dishes.

16. Middle age is when broadness of the mind and narrowness of the waist change places.

17. Opportunities always look bigger going than coming.

18. Junk is something you've kept for years and throw away three weeks before you need it.

19. The most destructive force in the universe is gossip.

20. Experience is a wonderful thing. It enables you to recognize a mistake when you make it again.

21. By the time you can make ends meet, they move the ends.

22. People who want to share their religious views with you almost never want you to share yours with them.

23. Some one who thinks logically provides a nice contrast to the real world.

24. There is a very fine line between 'hobby' and 'mental illness'.

25. Never be afraid to try something new. Remember that a lone amateur built the Ark. A large group of profess-ionals built the *Titanic*.

More Life Rules

1. I can only please one person per day. Today is not your day. Tomorrow is not looking good either.

2. I love deadlines. I especially like the whooshing sound they make as they go flying by.

3. Tell me what you need, and I'll tell you how to get along without it.

4. Accept that some days you are the pigeon and some days the statue.

5. Needing someone is like needing a parachute. If he/she isn't there the first time, chances are you won't be needing him/her again. . .

6. I don't have an attitude problem; you have a perception problem.

7. Last night I lay in bed looking up at the stars in the sky, and I thought to myself, where the heck is the ceiling?

8. My reality check bounced.

9. On the keyboard of life, always keep one finger on the Escape key.

10. I don't suffer from stress. I am a carrier.

11. You are slower than a herd of turtles stampeding through peanut butter.

12. Do not meddle in the affairs of dragons, because you are crunchy and taste good with ketchup.

13. Everybody is somebody else's weirdo.

14. Never argue with an idiot. They drag you down to their level, then beat you with experience.

15. A pat on the back is only a few inches from a kick in the butt.

16. Don't be irreplaceable – if you can't be replaced, you can't be promoted.

17. After any salary raise, you will have less money at the end of the month than you did before.

18. The more crap you put up with, the more crap you are going to get.

19. You can go anywhere you want, if you look serious and carry a clipboard.

20. Eat one live toad the first thing in the morning and nothing worse will happen to you the rest of the day.

21. If it wasn't for the last minute, nothing would get done.

22. When you don't know what to do, walk fast and look worried.

23. Following the rules will not get the job done.

24. When confronted by a difficult problem, you can solve it more easily by reducing it to the question, "How would the Lone Ranger[71] handle this?"

Additional Practical Life Rules

Sometimes, we just need to remember what the rules of life really are.

1. You only need two tools: WD-40®[72] and Duct Tape®.[73] If it doesn't move and should, use the WD-40®. If it shouldn't move and does, use the duct tape.

2. Remember: everyone seems normal until you get to know them.

3. Never pass up an opportunity to go to the bathroom.

4. If you woke up breathing, congratulations! You get another chance.

5. And finally, be really nice to your family and friends, you never know when you might need them to empty your bedpan.

Thoughts for the Day

(Authors various but anonymous)

1. Never take life too seriously. Nobody gets out alive anyway.

2. Life is sexually transmitted.

3. Good health is merely the slowest possible rate at which one can die.

4. Men have two emotions: hungry and horny. If you see him without an erection, make him a sandwich.

5. Give a person a fish and you feed them for a day; teach a person to use the Internet and they won't bother you for weeks.

6. Health nuts are going to feel stupid someday, lying in hospitals dying of nothing.

7. Whenever I feel blue, I start breathing again.

8. All of us could take a lesson from the weather. It pays no attention to criticism.

9. Why does a slight tax increase cost you two hundred dollars and a substantial tax cut saves you thirty cents?

10. In the sixties people took acid to make the world weird. Now the world is weird and people take Prozac® to make it normal.

11. Politics is supposed to be the second-oldest profession. I have come to realize that it bears a very close resemblance to the first.

12. Some people are like a Slinky®[74]. . . not really good for anything, but you still can't help but smile when you see one tumble down the stairs.

13. You read about terrorists; most of them went to the U.S. legally, but they hung around on these expired visas, some as long as ten to fifteen years. Now, compare that to Blockbuster®;[75] you are two days late with a video and those people are all over you. We should put Blockbuster® in charge of Homeland Security.

14. We know exactly where one cow with mad-cow-disease is located among the millions and millions of cows in America but we haven't got a clue as to where thousands of illegal immigrants are located. Maybe we should put the Department of Agriculture in charge of immigration.

Modern Philosophy

1. If at first you don't succeed, destroy all evidence that you tried.

2. A conclusion is the place where you got tired of thinking.

3. Experience is something you don't get until just after you need it.

4. For every action, there is an equal and opposite criticism.

5. He who hesitates is probably right.

6. Never do card tricks for the group you play poker with.

7. No one is listening until you make a mistake.

8. Success always occurs in private, and failure in full view.

9. The colder the X-ray table, the more of your body is required on it.

10. The hardness of the butter is proportional to the softness of the bread.

11. To steal ideas from one person is plagiarism; to steal from many is research.

12. To succeed in politics, it is often necessary to rise above your principles.

13. Two wrongs are only the beginning.

14. You never really learn to swear until you learn to drive. (The corollary is: You never learn to pray until your kids learn to drive!)

15. The problem with the gene pool is that there is no lifeguard.

16. Monday is an awful way to spend 1/7th of your life.

17. The sooner you fall behind, the more time you'll have to catch up.

Mean People

When you have to put up with mean people,

Think of them as sandpaper.

They may scratch you,

Rub you the wrong way

But eventually...

YOU end up smooth and polished.

And the sandpaper...?

It'd be worn out and ugly!

Makes you think, doesn't it?

Home Remedies

(Not to be tried!)

1. If you are choking on an ice cube, don't panic! Simply pour a cup of boiling water down your throat and presto! The blockage will be almost instantly removed.

2. Clumsy? Avoid cutting yourself while slicing vegetables by getting someone else to hold them while you chop away.

3. Avoid arguments with the Mrs. about lifting the toilet seat by simply using the sink.

4. For high blood pressure sufferers: just cut yourself and bleed for a few minutes, thus reducing the pressure in your veins.

5. A mouse trap, placed on top of your alarm clock, will prevent you from rolling over and going back to sleep after you hit the snooze button.

6. If you have a bad cough, take a large dose of laxatives, then you will be too afraid to cough.

7. Have a bad toothache? Smash your thumb with a hammer and you will forget about the toothache.

Twenty Great One-Liners

1. Regular naps prevent old age. . . especially if you take them while driving.

2. Having one child makes you a parent; having two makes you a referee.

3. Marriage is a relationship in which one person is always right and the other is the husband!

4. They said we should all pay our tax with a smile. I tried – but they wanted cash.

5. A child's greatest period of growth is the month after you've purchased new clothes.

6. Don't feel bad. . . a lot of people have no talent.

7. Don't marry the person you want to live with, marry the one you cannot live without. . . but whatever you do, you'll regret it later.

8. You can't buy love. . . but you pay heavily for it.

9. True friends stab you in the front.

10. Forgiveness is giving up my right to hate you for hurting me.

11. Bad politicians are elected by good citizens who don't vote.

12. Laziness is nothing more than the habit of resting before you get tired.

13. My wife and I always compromise. I admit I'm wrong and she agrees with me.

14. Those who can't laugh at themselves leave the job to others.

15. Ladies first. . . pretty ladies sooner.

16. It doesn't matter how often a married man changes his job, he still ends up with the same boss.

17. They call our language the mother tongue because the father seldom gets to speak.

18. Saving is smart. . . especially when your parents have done it for you.

19. Wise men talk because they have something to say; fools talk because they have to say something.

20. Real friends are the ones who survive transitions between address books.

More One-Liners

1. My husband and I divorced over religious differences. He thought he was God and I didn't!

2. I don't suffer from insanity, I enjoy every minute of it.

3. I work hard because millions on Welfare depend on me!

4. Don't take life too seriously, you won't get out alive.

5. You're just jealous because the voices only talk to me.

6. Beauty is in the eye of the beer holder.

7. Earth is the insane asylum for the universe.

8. I'm not a complete idiot, some parts are missing.

9. Out of my mind. Back in five minutes.

10. God must love stupid people; He made so many.

11. The gene pool could use a little chlorine.

12. Consciousness: that annoying time between naps.

13. Ever stop to think, and forget to start again?

14. Wrinkled was not one of the things I wanted to be when I grew up.

15. Computer programmers don't byte, they nibble a bit.

16. Finally twenty-one, and legally able to do everything I've been doing since fifteen.

17. Failure is not an option. It comes bundled with the software.

18. My wild oats have turned to shredded wheat.

19. A journey of a thousand miles begins with a cash advance from the ATM[76] machine.

20. Stupidity is not a handicap. Park elsewhere!

21. They call it PMS (Premenstrual Syndrome) because Mad Cow Disease was already taken.

22. Police station toilet stolen. . . Cops have nothing to go on.

23. A picture is worth a thousand words, but it uses up a thousand times the memory.

24. The Meek shall inherit the Earth, after we're through with it.

25. I didn't lose my mind. I sold it on e-Bay®!

26. Being "over the hill" is much better than being under it.

27. Procrastinate now!

28. A hangover is the wrath of grapes.

29. He who dies with the most toys is nonetheless dead.

30. Ham and eggs – a day's work for a chicken, a lifetime commitment for a pig.

31. The trouble with life is there's no background music.

32.   The original point and click interface was a Smith & Wesson®.

Natural Highs

1.   Falling in love.

2.   Laughing so hard your face hurts.

3.   A hot shower.

4.   No lines at the supermarket

5.   A special glance.

6.   Getting mail

7.   Taking a drive on a pretty road.

8.   Hearing your favorite song on the radio.

9.   Lying in bed listening to the rain outside.

10.   Hot towels fresh out of the dryer.

11.   Finding the sweater you want is on sale for half price.

12.   Chocolate milkshake (or vanilla) (or strawberry).

13.   A long distance phone call.

14.   A bubble bath.

15.   Giggling.

16.   A good conversation.

17.   The beach

18.   Finding a twenty dollar bill in your coat from last winter.

19.   Laughing at yourself.

20.   Midnight phone calls that last for hours.

21.   Running through sprinklers.

22.   Laughing for absolutely no reason at all.

23.   Having someone tell you that you're beautiful.

24. Laughing at an inside joke.

25. Friends.

26. Accidentally overhearing someone say something nice about you.

27. Waking up and realizing you still have a few hours left to sleep.

28. Your first kiss (either the very first or with a new partner).

29. Making new friends or spending time with old ones.

30. Playing with a new puppy.

31. Having someone play with your hair.

32. Sweet dreams.

33. Hot chocolate.

34. Road trips with friends.

35. Swinging on swings.

36. Wrapping presents under the Christmas tree while eating cookies and drinking your favorite tipple.

37. Song lyrics printed inside your new CD so you can sing along without feeling stupid.

38. Going to a really good concert.

39. Making eye contact with a cute stranger

40. Winning a really competitive game.

41. Making chocolate chip cookies.

42. Having your friends send you home-made cookies.

43. Spending time with close friends.

44. Seeing smiles and hearing laughter from your friends.

45. Holding hands with someone you care about.

46. Running into an old friend and realizing that some things (good or bad) never change.

47. Riding the best roller coasters over and over.

48. Watching the expression on someone's face as they open a much desired present from you.

49. Watching the sunrise.

50. Getting out of bed every morning and being grateful for another beautiful day.

(Note: I suspect this has been sponsored by a chocolate company).

Why ????

(Author Unknown)

1. Why do we press harder on a remote control when we know the batteries are flat?

2. Why do banks charge a fee on "insufficient funds" when they know there aren't enough?

3. Why does someone believe you when you say there are four billion stars, but check when you say the paint is wet?

4. Why doesn't glue stick to the bottle?

5. Why do they use sterilized needles for death by lethal injection?

6. Why doesn't Tarzan have a beard?

7. Why does Superman stop bullets with his chest, but ducks when you throw a revolver at him?

8. Why do Kamikaze pilots wear helmets?

9. Whose idea was it to put an 's' in the word 'lisp'?

10.   What is the speed of darkness?

11.   Are there especially reserved parking spaces for 'normal' people at the Special Olympics?

12.   If you send someone 'Styrofoam®,[77] how do you pack it?

13.   If the temperature is zero outside today and it's going to be twice as cold tomorrow, how cold will it be?

14.   If people evolved from apes, why are there still apes?

15.   If it's true that we are here to help others, what are the others doing here?

16.   Do married people live longer than single ones or does it only seem longer?

17.   If someone with a split personality threatens to commit suicide, is it a hostage situation?

More Sensible Questions

(Author Unknown)

1.   Can you cry under water?

2.   How important does a person have to be before they are considered assassinated instead of just murdered?

3.   Once you're in heaven, do you get stuck wearing the clothes you were buried in for eternity?

4.   Why does a round pizza come in a square box?

5.   What disease did cured ham actually have?

6.   How is it that we put Man on the Moon before we figured out it would be a good idea to put wheels on luggage?

7. Why is it that people say they "slept like a baby" when babies wake up like every two hours?

8. If a deaf person has to go to court, is it still called a hearing?

9. Why are you IN a movie, but you're ON TV?

10. Why do people pay to go up tall buildings and then put money in binoculars to look at things on the ground?

11. Why do doctors leave the room while you change? They're going to see you naked anyway.

12. Why is "bra" singular and "panties" plural?

13. Why do toasters always have a setting that burns the toast to a horrible crisp, which no decent human being would eat?

14. Can a hearse carrying a corpse drive in the carpool lane?

15. Why does Goofy stand erect while Pluto remains on all fours? They're both dogs!

16. If corn oil is made from corn, and vegetable oil is made from vegetables, what is baby oil made from?

17. Why do they call it an asteroid when it's outside the hemisphere, but call it a hemorrhoid when it's in your butt?

18. Did you ever notice that when you blow in a dog's face, he gets mad at you, but when you take him for a car ride, he sticks his head out the window?

Corporate Lessons

Corporate Lesson 1

A man is getting into the shower just as his wife is finishing up her shower when the doorbell rings. After a few seconds of arguing over which one should go and answer the doorbell, the wife gives up, quickly wraps herself up in a towel and runs downstairs. When she opens the door, there stands Bob, the next door neighbor. Before she says a word, Bob says, "I'll give you eight hundred dollars to drop that towel that you have on." After thinking for a moment, the woman drops her towel and stands naked in front of Bob. After a few seconds, Bob hands her eight hundred dollars and leaves. Confused, but excited about her good fortune, the woman wraps back up in the towel and goes back upstairs. When she gets back to the bathroom, her husband asks from the shower, "Who was that?" "It was Bob the next door neighbor," she replies. "Great!" the husband says, "Did he say anything about the eight hundred dollars he owes me?"

Moral of the story: if you share critical information pertaining to credit and risk in time with your stakeholders, you may be in a position to prevent avoidable exposure.

Corporate Lesson 2

A priest is driving along and sees a nun on the side of the road. He stops and offers her a lift which she accepts. She gets in and crossed her legs, forcing her gown to open and reveal a lovely leg. The priest has a look and nearly has an accident. After controlling the car, he stealthily slides his hand up her leg. The nun looks at him and immediately says, "Father, remember Psalm 129?" The priest is flustered and apologizes profusely. He forces himself to remove his hand. Changing gear, he lets his hand slide up her leg again. The nun once again says, "Father, remember Psalm 129?" Once again the priest apologizes, "Sorry sister, but the flesh is weak." Arriving at the convent, the nun gets out, gives him a meaningful glance and goes on her way. On his arrival at the church, the priest rushes to retrieve a bible and looks up Psalm 129. It says, "Go forth and seek, further up, you will find glory."

Moral of the story: always be well informed in your job, or you might miss a great opportunity.

Corporate Lesson 3

A sales representative, an administration clerk, and the manager are walking to lunch when they find an antique oil lamp. They rub it and a genie comes out in a puff of smoke. The genie says, "I usually only grant three wishes, so I'll give each of you just one." "Me first! Me first!" says the admin clerk. "I want to be in the Bahamas, driving a speedboat, without a care in the world." Poof! She's gone. In astonishment, "Me next! Me next!" says the sales rep. "I want to be in Hawaii, relaxing on the beach with my personal masseuse, an endless supply of pina coladas, and the love of my life." Poof! He's gone. "OK, you're up," the genie says to the manager. The manager says, "I want those two back in the office after lunch."

Moral of the story: always let your boss have the first say.

Corporate Lesson 4

A crow is sitting on a tree, doing nothing all day. A small rabbit sees the crow, and asks him, "Can I also sit like you and do nothing all day long?" The crow answers, "Sure, why not." So, the rabbit sits on the ground below the crow, and rests. All of a sudden a fox appears, jumps on the rabbit, and eats it.

Moral of the story: to be sitting and doing nothing, you must be sitting very, very high up.

Corporate Lesson 5

A turkey is chatting with a bull. "I would love to be able to get to the top of that tree," sighs the turkey, "but I haven't got the energy." "Well, why don't you nibble on some of my droppings?" replies the bull. "They're packed with nutrients." The turkey pecks at a lump of dung and finds that it actually gives him enough strength to reach the lowest branch of the tree. The next day, after eating some more dung, he reaches the second branch. Finally, after a fourth night, there he is proudly perched at the top of the tree. Soon he is spotted by a farmer, who promptly shoots the turkey out of the tree.

Moral of the story: bullshit might get you to the top, but it won't keep you there.

Corporate Lesson 6

A little bird is flying south for the winter. It is so cold the bird freezes and falls to the ground in a large field. While it is lying there, a cow comes by and drops some dung on it. As the frozen bird lays there in the pile of cow dung, it begins to realize how warm it is. The dung is actually thawing him out! He lays there all warm and happy, and soon begins to sing for joy. A passing cat hears the bird singing and comes to investigate. Following the sound, the cat discovers the bird under the pile of cow dung, and promptly digs him out and eats him.

Moral of the story: not everyone who shits on you is your enemy; not everyone who gets you out of shit is your friend; and when you're in deep shit, it's best to keep your mouth shut.

How to Get Rid of Telemarketing and Junk Mail

For Getting Rid of Telemarketers:
Three Little Words That Work!

The three little words are: "Hold on, please." Saying this, while putting down your phone and walking off (instead of hanging-up immediately) would make each telemarketing call so much more time-consuming that boiler room sales would grind to a halt. Then when you eventually hear the phone company's "beep-beep-beep" tone, you know it's time to go back and hang up your handset, which has efficiently completed its task. These three little words will help eliminate telephone soliciting.

Do you ever get those annoying phone calls with no one on the other end? This is a telemarketing technique where a machine makes phone calls and records the time of day when a

Capitalism

person answers the phone. This technique is used to determine the best time of day for a "real" sales person to call back and get someone at home. What you can do after answering, if you notice there is no one there, is to immediately start hitting your # button on the phone, six or seven times, as quickly as possible. This confuses the machine that made the call and it kicks your number out of their system. Gosh, what a shame not to have your name in their system any longer!

Junk Mail Help

When you get "ads" enclosed with your phone or utility bill, return these "ads" with your payment. Let the sending companies throw their own junk mail away. When you get those "pre-approved" letters in the mail for everything from credit cards to second mortgages and similar type junk, do not throw away the return envelope. Most of these come with postage-paid return envelopes, right? It costs them more than the regular postage "IF" and when they receive them back. It costs them nothing if you throw them away! The postage was around fifty cents before the last increase and it is according to the weight. In that case, why not get rid of some of your other junk mail and put it in these cool little, postage-paid return envelopes?

Send an ad for your local chimney cleaner to American Express®. Send a pizza coupon to Citibank®. If you didn't get anything else that day, then just send them their blank application back! If you want to remain anonymous, just make sure your name isn't on anything you send them. You can even send the envelope back empty if you want to just to keep them guessing! It still costs them regular postage. The banks and credit card companies are currently getting a lot of their own junk back in the mail, but folks, we need to OVERWHELM them. Let's let them know what it's like to get lots of junk mail, and best of all they're paying for it. . . twice! Let's help keep our postal service busy since they are saying that e-mail is cutting into their business profits, and that's why they need to increase postage costs again. You get the idea! If enough people follow these tips, it will work...

The Best Lessons I have EVER Learned!

(Author Anonymous)

If your father is a poor man, it is your fate
but if your father-in-law is a poor man, it's your stupidity.

I was born intelligent. Education ruined me.

Practice makes perfect. . . but nobody's perfect. . . so why practice?

If it's true that we are here to help others, then what exactly are the others here for?

Since light travels faster than sound, people appear bright until you hear them speak.

How come "abbreviated" is such a long word?

Money is not everything. There's Mastercard® & Visa®.

One should love animals. They are so tasty.

Behind every successful man, there is a woman.
And behind every unsuccessful man, there are two.

Every man should marry. After all, happiness is
not the only thing in life.

The wise never marry. And when they marry they
become otherwise.

Success is a relative term. It brings so many relatives.

Never put off the work till tomorrow what you
can put off today.

"Your future depends on your dreams." So go to sleep.

There should be a better way to start a day than
waking up every morning.

"Hard work never killed anybody." But why take the risk?

"Work fascinates me." I can look at it for hours.

God made relatives. Thank God we can choose our friends.

The more you learn, the more you know. The more you know,
the more you forget.
The more you forget, the less you know. So why learn?

A bus station is where a bus stops. A train station is where a
train stops.
On my desk, I have a work station.. . . what more can I say?

11) ABOUT GETTING OLD

Age-Activated Attention Deficit Disorder

Recently, I was diagnosed with Age-Activated Attention
Deficit Disorder (AAADD). This is how it manifests itself. I
decide to wash my car. As I start toward the garage, I notice that
there is mail on the hall table. I decide to go through the mail
before I wash the car. I lay my car keys down on the table, put
the junk mail in the trash can under the table, and notice that the
trash can is full. So, I decide to put the bills back on the table
and take out the trash first. But then I think, since I'm going to
be near the mailbox when I take out the trash anyway, I may as
well pay the bills first. I take my check book off the table, and see
that there is only one check left. My extra checks are in my desk
in the study, so I go to my desk where I find the can of Coke® that
I had been drinking. I'm going to look for my checks, but first I
need to push the Coke® aside so that I don't accidentally knock
it over. I see that the Coke® is getting warm, and I decide I should

put it in the refrigerator to keep it cold. As I head toward the kitchen with the Coke® a vase of flowers on the counter catches my eye: they need to be watered. I set the Coke® down on the counter, and I discover my reading glasses that I've been searching for all morning. I decide I'd better put them back on my desk, but first I'm going to water the flowers. I set the glasses back down on the counter, fill a container with water and suddenly I spot the TV remote control. Someone left it on the kitchen table. I realize that tonight when we go to watch TV, I will be looking for the remote, but I won't remember that it's on the kitchen table, so I decide to put it back in the den where it belongs, but first I'll water the flowers. I splash some water on the flowers, but most of it spills on the floor. So, I set the remote back down on the table, get some towels and wipe up the spill. Then I head down the hall trying to remember what I was planning to do. At the end of the day: the car isn't washed, the bills aren't paid, there is a warm can of Coke® sitting on the counter, the flowers aren't watered, there is still only one check in my checkbook, I can't find the remote, I can't find my glasses, and I don't remember what I did with the car keys. Then when I try to figure out why nothing got done today, I'm really baffled because I know I was busy all day long, and I'm really tired. I realize this is a serious problem, and I'll try to get some help for it, but first I'll check my e-mail. Do me a favor, will you? Forward this message to everyone you know, because I don't remember to whom it has been sent. Don't laugh – if this isn't you yet, your day is coming!

GROWING OLDER IS MANDATORY.

GROWING UP IS OPTIONAL.

LAUGHING AT YOURSELF IS THERAPEUTIC!

Proof You Are Aging in Twenty-Five Points

1. Your home plants are alive, and you can't smoke any of them.
2. Making love in twin beds is for you out of the question.
3. You are storing more food than drinks in your fridge.
4. 6:00 a.m. is the time when you get up and not when you go to bed.
5. You can hear your favorite song in an elevator.
6. You watch the Weather Channel®.
7. Your friends get married and get a divorce instead of "dating and splitting."
8. Your vacation time goes from one hundred and thirty days to fourteen.
9. Wearing a pair of jeans and a sweater is no long considered as "dressing up."
10. You are the one who calls the police because the %&@# next-door youngsters won't turn the music down.
11. Older parents feel comfortable telling dirty jokes in your presence.
12. You forgot the closing time of the fast-food restaurant around the corner.
13. Your car insurance is cheaper and your car monthly payments are more expensive.

14. You feed your dog organic food and not McDonald's® leftovers.

15. Sleeping on the couch gives you a backache.

16. You take naps.

17. Instead of starting the evening with a movie and restaurant, the evening consists in a movie and restaurant.

18. Eating fried chicken at 3 o'clock in the morning makes you feel sick instead of full.

19. You go to the drugstore for Panadol® and Alka-Seltzer® instead of condoms and pregnancy tests.

20. A good Bordeaux costs no longer fifteen dollars a bottle but fifteen dollars a glass.

21. You have your breakfast at breakfast time.

22. "I can't drink as much as I used to" replaces "I'll never drink that much."

23. Ninety percent of the time you spent in front of a computer screen is really to work.

24. You drink cocktails at home to save before going out to the bar.

25. When you learn your friend is pregnant, you congratulate her instead of asking, "Hell, how did it happen?"

Grandpa

A small boy is lost at a large shopping mall. He approaches a uniformed policeman and says, "I've lost my grandpa." The cop asks, "What's he like?" The little boy replies, "Jack Daniels® and women with big boobs."

Wisdom from Grandpa

To all Older Wiser Laughin' Souls (OWLS)

1. A foolish husband says to his wife, "Honey, you stick to the washin', ironin', cookin' and scrubbin'. No wife of mine is gonna work."
2. Ah, being young is beautiful, but being old is comfortable.
3. Eventually you will reach a point when you stop lying about your age and start bragging about it.
4. How old would you be if you didn't know how old you are?
5. I don't know how I got over the hill without getting to the top.
6. If a man has enough horse sense to treat his wife like a thoroughbred, she will never turn into an old nag.
7. If you don't learn to laugh at trouble, you won't have anything to laugh at when you are old.
8. Long ago when men cursed and beat the ground with sticks, it was called witchcraft. Today it's called golf.
9. Many girls like to marry a military man – he can cook, sew, and make beds and is in good health, and he's already used to taking orders.
10. Old age is when former classmates are so grey and wrinkled and bald, they don't recognize you.
11. On anniversaries, the wise husband always forgets the past – but never the present.

12. One must wait until evening to see how splendid the day has been.

13. One of the many things no one tells you about aging is that it is such a nice change from being young.

14. Some people try to turn back their odometers. Not me, I want people to know why I look this way. I've traveled a long way and some of the roads weren't paved.

15. The bonds of matrimony are a good investment only when the interest is kept up.

16. The older we get, the fewer things seem worth waiting in line for.

17. Too many couples marry for better or for worse, but not for good.

18. Trouble in marriage often starts when a man gets so busy earnin' his salt that he forgets his sugar.

19. When a man marries a woman, they become one; but the trouble starts when they try to decide which one.

20. When you are dissatisfied and would like to go back to your youth. . . Remember about Algebra.

21. Whether a man winds up with a nest egg, or a goose egg, depends a lot on the kind of chick he marries.

22. You know you are getting old when everything either dries up or leaks.

23. And finally: If you don't learn to laugh at trouble, you won't have anything to laugh at when you are old.

Quotes by Bob Hope

ON TURNING 70: "You still chase women, but only downhill."

ON TURNING 80: "That's the time of your life when even your birthday suit needs pressing."

ON TURNING 90: "You know you're getting old when the candles cost more than the cake."

ON TURNING 100: "I don't feel old. In fact I don't feel anything until noon. Then it's time for my nap."

Grandma

The doctor that has been seeing an eighty-year old woman for most of her life finally retires. At her next checkup, the new doctor tells her to bring a list of all the medicines that have been prescribed for her. As the young doctor is looking through these, his eyes grow wide as he realizes she had a prescription for birth control pills. "Mrs. Smith, do you realize these are BIRTH CONTROL pills?" "Yes, they help me sleep at night." "Mrs. Smith, I assure you there is absolutely NOTHING in these that could possibly help you sleep!" She reaches out and pat the young Doctor's knee. "Yes, dear, I know that. But every morning, I grind one up and mix it in the glass of orange juice that my sixteen-year old granddaughter drinks. . . and believe me, it helps me sleep at night."

Getting Old?

I feel like my body has gotten totally out of shape, so I got my doctor's permission to join a fitness club and start exercising. I decided to take an aerobics class for seniors. I bent, twisted, gyrated, jumped up and down, and perspired for an hour. But, by the time I got my leotards on, the class was over.

■

Reporters interviewing a 104-year-old woman: "And what do you think is the best thing about being 104?" the reporter asked. She simply replied, "No peer pressure."

■

Just before the funeral services, the undertaker comes up to the very elderly widow and asks, "How old was your husband?" "Ninety-eight," she replies. "Two years older than me." "So you're ninety-six," the undertaker comments. She responds, "Hardly worth going home, is it?"

■

I've sure gotten old! I've had two bypass surgeries, a hip replacement, new knees; fought prostate cancer and diabetes. I'm half blind, can't hear anything quieter than a jet engine, take forty different medications that make me dizzy, winded, and subject to blackouts. Have bouts with dementia. Have poor circulation; hardly feel my hands and feet anymore. Can't remember if I'm eighty-five or ninety-two. Have lost all my friends. But, thank God, I still have my driver's license.

■

An elderly woman decides to prepare her will and tells her

preacher she has two final requests. First, she wants to be cremated, and second, she wants her ashes scattered over Wal-Mart®.[78] "Wal-Mart®?" the preacher exclaims. "Why Wal-Mart®?" "Then I'll be sure my daughters visit me twice a week."

■

My memory's not as sharp as it used to be. Also, my memory's not as sharp as it used to be.

■

Know how to prevent sagging? Just eat till the wrinkles fill out.

■

I'm getting into swing dancing. Not on purpose. Some parts of my body are just prone to swinging.

■

It's scary when you start making the same noises as your coffeemaker.

■

These days about half the stuff in my shopping cart says, "For fast relief."

*

Don't think of it as getting hot flashes. Think of it as your inner child playing with matches.

■

Don't let aging get you down. It's too hard to get back up!

■

Remember: you don't stop laughing because you grow old. You grow old because you stop laughing.

(2007) New Year's Eve Toast

Milords, Ladies and Gentlemen, kindly raise your GLASSES IN SPECIAL TRIBUTE TO ALL THE GIRLS WE'VE LOVED BEFORE...

How's This For Depressing? (Apologies for the indiscretion)

Julie Christie, Ann-Margret: 66

Elke Sommer, Jill St. John: 67

Stella Stevens: 70

Ursula Andress: 71

Julie Andrews: 72

Brigitte Bardot, Sophia Loren, Barbara Eden: 73

Joan Collins, Debra Padget, Kim Novak: 74

Debbie Reynolds, Liz Taylor: 75

Angie Dickinson, Leslie Caron, Rita Moreno: 76

Jean Simmons, Jane Powell: 78

Shirley Temple: 79

Gina Lollobrigida, Patti Page: 80

Doris Day: 83

Esther Williams: 84

Kay Starr, Gale Storm: 85

Jane Russell: 86

Lena Horne: 90

UNBELIEVEABLE: HOW IN THE WORLD DID THEY GET OLD AND WE DIDN'T???

What is Old?

"Old" is when:

1. Your sweetie says, "Let's go upstairs and make love," and you answer, "Pick one, I can't do both!"

2. Your friends compliment you on your new alligator shoes and you're barefoot.

3. A sexy babe catches your eye and your pacemaker opens the garage door.

4. Seeing a bra-less bather pulls all the wrinkles out of your face.

5. You don't care where your spouse goes, just as long as you don't have to go along.

6. You are cautioned to slow down by. . . the doctor instead of by the police.

7. "Getting lucky" means you find your car in the parking lot.

How Old?

A woman decides to have a facelift for her birthday. She spends five thousand dollars, has the surgery, and is very satisfied with the results. On her first day out, she stops at a newsstand to buy a newspaper. Before leaving she says to the clerk, "I hope you don't mind my asking, but how old do you think I am?" "About thirty-two," is the reply. "I'm exactly forty-seven," the woman says happily. A little while later she goes into McDonald's® and asks the counter girl the very same question. She replies, "I guess about twenty-nine." "No, I'm forty-seven."

Now, she's feeling really good about herself. She stops in a drugstore on her way down the street. She goes up to the counter to get some mints and asks the clerk this burning question. The clerk responds, "Oh, I'd say thirty." Again she proudly responds, "I am forty-seven , but, thank you." While waiting for the bus to go home, she asks an old man the same question. He replies, "Lady, I'm seventy-eight and my eyesight is going. Although, when I was young, there was a sure way to tell how old a woman was. It sounds very forward, but it requires you to let me put my hands under your bra. Then I can tell you exactly how old you are." They wait in silence on the empty street until curiosity gets the best of her. She finally blurts out, "What the heck, go ahead." He slips both of his hands under her blouse and under her bra and begins to feel around very slowly and carefully. After a couple of minutes of this, she says, "Okay, okay, how old am I?" He completes one last squeeze of her breasts, removes his hands, and says, "Madam, you are forty-seven." Stunned and amazed, the woman says, "That was incredible, how could you tell?" The old man replies, "Promise you won't get mad?" "No, I won't get mad", she says. He replies, "I was behind you in line at McDonald's®."

Old and Young Chicken

A farmer goes out one day and buys a brand new stud rooster for his chicken coop. The new rooster struts over to the old rooster and says, "OK, old fart, time for you to retire." The old rooster replies, "Come on, surely you cannot handle ALL of these chickens. Look what it has done to me. Can't you just let me have the two old hens over in the corner?" The young rooster says, "Beat it! You are washed up and I am taking over." The old rooster says, "I tell you what, young stud. I will race you around the farmhouse. Whoever wins gets the exclusive domain over the entire chicken coop." The young rooster laughs: "You know you don't stand a chance old man, so just to be fair I will give you a head start." The old rooster takes off running. About fifteen seconds later the young rooster takes off running after him. They round the front porch of the farmhouse and the young rooster has closed the gap. He is already about five inches behind the old rooster and gaining fast. The farmer, meanwhile, is sitting in his usual spot of the front porch when he sees the roosters running by. He grabs up his shotgun and BOOM! He blows the young rooster to bits. The farmer sadly shakes his head and says, "Damn it. . . third gay rooster I bought this month."

Remember the quote: "Age, experience, and treachery will always overcome youth and ambition."

Dinner

Two elderly ladies meet at the launderette after not seeing one another for some time. After inquiring about each other's health one asks how the other's husband is doing. "Oh! Ted died last week. He went out to the garden to dig up a cabbage for dinner, had a heart attack and dropped down dead right there in the middle of the vegetable patch!" "Oh dear! I'm very sorry." Replies her friend. "What did you do?" "Opened a can of peas instead!"

News from Napa Valley

California vintners in the Napa Valley area that primarily produces Pinot Blanc and Pinot Grigio have developed a new hybrid grape that acts as an anti-diuretic and will reduce the number of trips an older person has to make to the bathroom during the night. They will be marketing the new wine as "Pinot More."

For Aging People

Now that I'm 'older' (but refuse to grow up),
here's what I've discovered:

1. I started out with nothing, and I still have most of it.
2. My wild oats have turned into prunes and All Bran®.[79]
3. I finally got my head together; now my body is falling apart.
4. Funny, I don't remember being absent minded. . .
5. All reports are in; life is now officially unfair.
6. If all is not lost, where is it?
7. It is easier to get older than it is to get wiser.
8. Funny, I don't remember being absent minded. . .
9. Some days you're the dog; some days you're the hydrant.
10. I wish the buck stopped here; I sure could use a few. . .
11. Kids in the back seat cause accidents.
12. Accidents in the back seat cause kids.
13. Funny, I don't remember being absent minded. . .
14. The only time the world beats a path to your door is when you're in the bathroom.

15. If God wanted me to touch my toes, he would have put them on my knees.

16. When I'm finally holding all the cards, why does everyone decide to play chess?

17. Funny, I don't remember being absent minded. . .

18. It's not hard to meet expenses. . . they're everywhere.

19. The only difference between a rut and a grave is the depth.

20. These days, I spend a lot of time thinking about the hereafter. I go somewhere to get something and then wonder what I'm here after.

21. Funny, I don't remember being… absent minded...

Bran Muffins

They are eighty-five years old, and have been married for sixty years. Though they are far from rich, they manage to get by because they watch their pennies. Though not young, they are both in very good health, largely due to the wife's insistence on healthy foods and exercise for the last two decades. One day, their good health doesn't help when they go on a rare vacation and their plane unfortunately crashes, sending them off to Heaven. They reach the Pearly Gates, and St. Peter escorts them inside. He takes them to a beautiful mansion, furnished in gold and fine silks, with a fully stocked kitchen and a waterfall in the master bath. A maid can be seen hanging their favorite clothes in the closet. They gasp in astonishment when St. Peter said, "Welcome to Heaven. This will be your home now." The old man asks Peter how much all this was going to cost. "Why, nothing," Peter replies, "Remember, this is your reward in Heaven." The old man looks out the window and right there he sees a championship golf course, finer and more beautiful than any ever-built on Earth. "What are the greens fees?" grumbled the old man. "This is Heaven," St. Peter replies. "You can play for free, every day, any time of day that you want." Next they go to the clubhouse and see the lavish buffet lunch, with every imaginable cuisine laid out before them, from seafood to steaks to exotic desserts, free flowing beverages. "Don't even ask," says St. Peter to the man. "This is Heaven, it is all free for you to enjoy." The old man looks around and glances nervously at his wife. "Well, where are the low fat and low cholesterol foods, and the decaffeinated tea?" he asks. "That's the best part," St. Peter replies. "You can eat and drink as much as you like of whatever you like, and you will never get fat or sick. This is Heaven!" The old man inquires, "No gym to work out at?" "Not unless you want to," is the answer. "No testing my sugar or blood pressure or..." "Never again. All you do here is enjoy yourself." The old man glares at his wife and says, "You and your f*@#in' bran muffins. We could have been here twenty years ago!"

Mirror

A woman, standing nude, looks in the bedroom mirror and says to her husband, "I look horrible, I feel fat and ugly – pay me a compliment." The husband replies, "Your eyesight's absolutely perfect."

People Over Thirty-Five Should Be Dead

Here's why. . .

According to today's regulators and bureaucrats, those of us who were kids in the forties, fifties, sixties, or even maybe (just maybe!) the early seventies probably shouldn't have survived.

1. Our baby cribs were covered with bright colored lead-based paint.

2. We had no childproof lids on medicine bottles, plug sockets, doors or cabinets, and when we rode our bikes, we had no helmets (not to mention the risks we took hitchhiking).

3. As children, we would ride in cars with no seatbelts or air bags. Riding in the back of a pick-up or truck on a warm day was always a special treat.

4. We drank water from the garden hose and not from a bottle. Horrors!

5. We ate cupcakes, bread and butter, and drank soda pop with sugar in it, but we were never overweight because we were always outside playing.

6. We shared one soft drink with four friends, from one bottle, and no one actually died from this.

7. We would spend hours building our go-carts out of scraps and then rode down the hill, only to find out we forgot the brakes. After running into the bushes a few times, we learned to solve the problem.

8. We would leave home in the morning and play all day, as long as we were back when the street lights came on.

9. No one was able to reach us all day. WE HAD NO MOBILE PHONES!!!!! Unthinkable!

10. We did not have Play Stations®, Nintendo 64®, X-Boxes®80, no video games at all, no ninety-nine channels on cable, video tape movies, surround sound, personal computers, Internet chat rooms or Facebook®.

11. We had friends! We went outside and found them.

12. We played brandy81 and sometimes the ball would really hurt.

13. We fell out of trees, got cut and broke bones and teeth, and there were no lawsuits from these accidents. They were accidents. No one was to blame but us. Remember accidents?

14. We had fights and punched each other and got black and blue and learned to get over it.

15. We made up games with sticks and tennis balls and ate worms, and although we were told it would happen, we did not poke out any eyes, nor did the worms live inside us forever.

16. We rode bikes or walked to a friend's home and knocked on the door, or rang the bell or just walked in and talked to them.

17. Football and netball clubs had tryouts and not everyone made the team. Those who didn't had to learn to deal with disappointment.

18. Some students weren't as smart as others, so they failed a grade and were held back to repeat the same grade. Tests were not adjusted for any reason.

19. Our actions were our own. Consequences were expected.

20. The idea of a parent bailing us out if we broke a law was unheard of. They actually sided with the law. Imagine that!

21. Our generation produced some of the best risk-takers and problem solvers and inventors, ever. The past fifty years have been an explosion of innovation and new ideas. We had freedom, failure, success and responsibility, and we learned how to deal with it all.

No Pun Jobs

My first job was working in an orange juice factory, but I got canned. I couldn't concentrate. Then I worked in the woods as a lumberjack, but I just couldn't hack it, so they gave me the axe. After that, I tried to be a tailor, but I just wasn't suited for it – mainly because it was a sew-sew job. Next, I tried working in a muffler factory, but that was too exhausting. Then, I tried to be a chef – figured it would add a little spice to my life, but I just didn't have the thyme. I attempted to be a deli worker, but any way I sliced it, I couldn't cut the mustard. My best job was being a musician, but eventually I found I wasn't noteworthy. I studied a long time to become a doctor, but I didn't have any patience. Next, was a job in a shoe factory. I tried but I just didn't fit in. I became a professional fisherman, but discovered that I couldn't live on my net income. I managed to get a good job working for a pool maintenance company, but the work was just too draining.

So then I got a job in a workout center, but they said I wasn't fit for the job. After many years of trying to find steady work, I finally got a job as a historian – until I realized there was no future in it. My last job was working in Starbucks®, but I had to quit because it was always the same old grind. SO, I TRIED RETIREMENT, AND FOUND I'M PERFECT FOR THE JOB!

Night Light

An eighty–year old man goes for a physical. All of his tests come back with normal results. The doctor says, "George, everything looks great. How are you doing mentally and emotionally? Are you at peace with God?" George replies, "God and I are tight. He knows I have poor eyesight, so he's fixed it so when I get up in the middle of the night to go to the bathroom, poof! The light goes on. When I'm done, poof! The light goes off." "Wow, that's incredible," the doctor says. A little later in the day, the doctor calls George's wife. "Ethel," he says, "George is doing fine! But I had to call you because I'm in awe of his relationship with God. Is it true that he gets up during the night and poof! The light goes on in the bathroom, and when he's done, poof! The light goes off?" "Oh my God!" Ethel exclaims. "He's peeing in the refrigerator again!"

Senior Driver

An older lady gets pulled over for speeding...
Older Woman: "Is there a problem, Officer?"
Officer: "Ma'am, you were speeding."

Older Woman: "Oh, I see."

Officer: "Can I see your license please?"

Older Woman: "I'd give it to you but I don't have one."

Officer: "Don't have one?"

Older Woman: "Lost it, four years ago for drunk driving."

Officer: "I see. . . Can I see your vehicle registration papers please?"

Older Woman: "I can't do that."

Officer: "Why not?"

Older Woman: "I stole this car."

Officer: "Stole it?"

Older Woman: "Yes, and I killed and hacked up the owner."

Officer: "You what?"

Older Woman: "His body parts are in plastic bags in the trunk if you want to see."

The Officer looks at the woman and slowly backs away to his car and calls for back up. Within minutes five police cars circle the car. A senior officer slowly approaches the car, clasping his half drawn gun.

Officer 2: "Ma'am, could you step out of your vehicle please!"

The woman steps out of her vehicle.

Older woman: "Is there a problem sir?"

Officer 2: "One of my officers told me that you have stolen this car and murdered the owner."

Older Woman: "Murdered the owner?"

Officer 2: "Yes, could you please open the trunk of your car, please?"

The woman opens the trunk, revealing nothing but an empty trunk.

Officer 2: "Is this your car, ma'am?"

Older Woman: "Yes, here are the registration papers."

The officer is quite stunned.

Officer 2: "One of my officers claims that you do not have a driving license."

The woman digs into her handbag and pulls out a clutch purse and hands it to the officer. The officer examines the license. He looks quite puzzled.

Officer 2: "Thank you ma'am, one of my officers told me you didn't have a license, that you stole this car, and that you murdered and hacked up the owner."

Older Woman: "Bet the liar told you I was speeding, too."

Walking

Walking can add minutes to your life. This enables you at eighty-five years old to spend an additional five months in a nursing home at five thousand dollars per month.

■

My grandmother started walking five miles a day when she was sixty. Now she's ninety-seven years old and we don't know where she is.

■

The only reason I would take up exercising is so that I could hear heavy breathing again.

■

I have to exercise early in the morning before my
brain figures out what I'm doing.

■

I like long walks, especially when they are taken
by people who annoy me.

■

I have flabby thighs, but fortunately my stomach covers them.

■

The advantage of exercising every day is that you die healthier.

■

If you are going to try cross-country skiing,
start with a small country.

■

I don't exercise because it makes the ice jump right out of my
glass of whisky.

How to Stay Young

(Advice from an Unknown Gerontologist)

1. Throw out non-essential numbers. This includes age,
   weight, and height. Let the doctors worry about them.
   That is why you pay them.
2. Keep only cheerful friends. The grouches pull you down.
   (Keep this in mind if you are one of those grouches!)
3. Keep learning: learn more about the computer, crafts,
   gardening, whatever. Never let the brain get idle. "An
   idle mind is the devil's workshop." And the devil's name
   is Alzheimer's!

4. Enjoy the simple things.

5. Laugh often, long and loud. Laugh until you gasp for breath. And if you have a friend who makes you laugh, spend lots and lots of time with her/him!

6. The tears happen: endure, grieve, and move on. The only person who is with us our entire life, is our self. LIVE while you are alive.

7. Surround yourself with what you love: whether it's family, pets, keepsakes, music, plants, hobbies, whatever. Your home is your refuge.

8. Cherish your health: if it is good, preserve it. If it is unstable, improve it. If it is beyond what you can improve, get help.

9. Don't take guilt trips. Take a trip to the mall, even to a foreign country, but NOT to where the guilt is.

10. Tell the people you love that you love them – at every opportunity.

Retirement

Working people frequently ask retired people what they do to make their days interesting. Well, for example, the other day my wife and I went into a shop. We were only in there for about five minutes. When we came out, there was a cop writing out a parking ticket. We went up to him and said, "Come on man, how about giving a senior citizen a break?" He ignored us and continued writing the ticket. I called him a Fascist. He glared at me and started writing another ticket for having worn tires. So my wife called him a shithead. He finished the second ticket and put it on the windshield with the first. Then he started writing a third ticket. This went on for about twenty minutes. The more we abused him, the more tickets he wrote. Personally, we didn't care. We came into town by bus. We try to have a little fun each day now that we're retired. It's important at our age.

The Senility Prayer

Lord, grant me the senility to forget the people I never liked anyway,

The good fortune to run into the ones I do,

And the eyesight to tell the difference.

12) DEFINITIONS AND PUNS

Alternative Definitions

(Suggested by anonymous readers to the
Washington Post *in 2005)*

1. **Coffee**: the person upon whom one coughs.
2. **Flabbergasted**: appalled over how much weight you have gained.
3. **Abdicate**: to give up all hope of ever having a flat stomach.
4. **Esplanade** (v.): to attempt an explanation while drunk.
5. **Willy-nilly** (adj.): impotent.
6. **Negligent** (adj.): describes a condition in which you absent-mindedly answer the door in your nightgown.
7. **Lymph** (v.): to walk with a lisp.
8. **Gargoyle** (n.): olive-flavored mouthwash.

9. **Flatulence** (n.): emergency vehicle that picks you up after you are run over by a steamroller.

10. **Balderdash** (n.): a rapidly receding hairline.

11. **Testicle** (n.): a humorous question on an exam.

12. **Rectitude** (n.): the formal, dignified bearing adopted by proctologists.

13. **Pokemon** (n): a Rastafarian proctologist.

14. **Oyster** (n.): a person who sprinkles his conversation with Yiddish-isms.

15. **Frisbeetarianism** (n.): the belief that, when you die, your soul flies up onto the roof and gets stuck there.

16. **Circumvent** (n.): an opening in the front of boxer shorts worn by Jewish men.

More Definitions

(Authors Anonymous)

1. **Atom Bomb**: An invention to end all inventions.

2. **Boss**: Someone who is early when you are late and late when you are early.

3. **Cigarette**: A pinch of tobacco rolled in paper with fire at one end and a fool at the other.

4. **Classic**: A book which people praise, but do not read.

5. **Committee**: Individuals who can do nothing individually and sit to decide that nothing can be done together.

6. **Compromise**: The art of dividing a cake in such a way that everybody believes he got the biggest piece.

7. **Conference**: The confusion of one man multiplied by the number present.

8. **Conference Room**: A place where everybody talks, nobody listens and everybody disagrees later on.

9. **Criminal**: A guy no different from the rest. . . except that he got caught.

10. **Dictionary**: A place where divorce comes before marriage.

11. **Diplomat**: A person who tells you to go to hell in such a way that you actually look forward to the trip.

12. **Divorce**: Future tense of marriage.

13. **Doctor**: A person who kills your ills by pills, and kills you with his bills.

14. **Ecstasy**: A feeling when you feel you are going to feel a feeling you have never felt before.

15. **Etc.**: A sign to make others believe that you know more than you actually do.

16. **Father**: A banker provided by nature.

17. **Lecture**: An art of transferring information from the notes of the lecturer to the notes of the students without passing through "the minds of either."

18. **Love affairs**: Something like cricket where one-day internationals are more popular than a five-day test.

19. **Marriage**: It's an agreement in which a man loses his bachelor degree and a woman gains her master.

20. **Miser**: A person who lives poor so that he can die rich.

21. **Opportunist**: A person who starts taking a bath if he accidentally falls into a river.

22. **Optimist**: A person who while falling from the Eiffel Tower says in midway "See I am not injured yet."

23. **Pessimist**: A person who says that O is the last letter in ZERO, Instead of the first letter in word OPPORTUNITY.

24. **Politician**: One who shakes your hand before elections and your confidence after.

25. **Smile**: A curve that can set a lot of things straight.

26. **Tears**: The hydraulic force by which masculine will-power is defeated by feminine water-power.

27. **Yawn**: The only time some married men ever get to open their mouth.

Financial Crisis Definitions

1. **CEO**: chief embezzlement officer.

2. **CFO**: corporate fraud officer.

3. **BULL MARKET**: A random market movement causing an investor to mistake himself for a financial genius.

4. **BEAR MARKET**: A six- to eighteen-month period when the kids get no allowance, the wife gets no jewelry, and the husband gets no sex.

5. **VALUE INVESTING**: The art of buying low and selling lower.

6. **P/E RATIO**: The percentage of investors wetting their pants as the market keeps crashing.

7. **BROKER**: What my broker has made me.

8. **STANDARD & POOR**: Your life in a nutshell.

9. **STOCK ANALYST**: Idiot who just downgraded your stock.

10. **STOCK SPLIT**: When your ex-wife and her lawyer split your assets equally between themselves.

11. **MARKET CORRECTION**: The day after you buy stocks.

12. **CASH FLOW**: The movement your money makes as it disappears down the toilet.

13. **INSTITUTIONAL INVESTOR**: Past year investor who's now locked up in a nuthouse.

14. **MOMENTUM INVESTING**: The fine art of buying high and selling low.

15. **"BUY, BUY"**: A flight attendant making market recommendations as you step off the plane.

16. **FINANCIAL PLANNER**: A guy who actually remembers his wallet when he runs to the 7-Eleven® for toilet paper and cigarettes.

17. **CALL OPTION**: Something people used to do with a telephone in ancient times before e-mail.

18. **YAHOO!®**: What you yell after selling all you owned to some poor sucker for two hundred and forty dollars per share.

19. **WINDOWS®**: What you jump out of when you're the sucker that bought Yahoo!® for two hundred and forty dollars per share.

20. **PROFIT**: Religious person who talks to God.

New Puns

1. Energizer® Bunny[82] arrested; charged with battery.

2. A man's home is his castle, in a manor of speaking.

3. A pessimist's blood type is always b-negative.

4. My wife really likes to make pottery, but to me it's just kiln time.

5. Dijon vu: the same mustard as before.

6. Practice safe eating: always use condiments.

7. I fired my masseuse today. She just rubbed me the wrong way.

8. A Freudian slip is when you say one thing but mean your mother.

9. Shotgun wedding: a case of wife or death.

10. I used to work in a blanket factory, but it folded.

11. I used to be a lumberjack, but I just couldn't hack it, so they gave me the axe.

12. If electricity comes from electrons, does that mean that morality comes from morons?

13. A man needs a mistress just to break the monogamy.

14. Marriage is the mourning after the knot before.

15. A hangover is the wrath of grapes.

16. Corduroy pillows are making headlines.

17. Is a book on voyeurism a peeping tome.

18. Banning the bra was a big flop.

19. Sea captains don't like crew cuts.

20. A successful diet is the triumph of mind over platter.

21. A gossip is someone with a great sense of rumor.

22. Without geometry, life is pointless.

23. When you dream in color, it's a pigment of your imagination.

24. Condoms should be used on every conceivable occasion.

25. Reading whilst sunbathing makes you well-red.

26. When two egotists meet, it's an I for an I.

Friday Groaners

1. A bicycle can't stand alone because it is two-tired.

2. What's the definition of a will? (It's a dead giveaway).

3. Time flies like an arrow. Fruit flies like a banana.

4. A backward poet writes inverse.

5. In democracy it's your vote that counts; in feudalism, it's your Count that votes.

6. A chicken crossing the road is poultry in motion.

7. If you don't pay your exorcist you get repossessed.

8. With her marriage she got a new name and a dress.

9. Show me a piano falling down a mine shaft and I'll show you A-flat minor.

10. When a clock is hungry it goes back four seconds.

11. The man who fell into an upholstery machine is fully recovered.

12. A grenade thrown into a pastry shop in France would result in a Napoleon Blownapart.

13. You feel stuck with your debt if you can't budge it.

14. He often broke into song because he couldn't find the key.

15. Every calendar's days are numbered.

16. A lot of money is tainted. 'Taint yours and 'taint mine.

17. A boiled egg in the morning is hard to beat.

18. A plateau is a high form of flattery.

19. The short fortune teller who escaped from prison was a small medium at large.

20. Those who get too big for their britches will be exposed in the end.

21. When you've seen one shopping center you've seen a mall.

22. Those who jump off a Paris bridge are in Seine.

23. When an actress saw her first strands of grey hair she thought she'd dye.

24. Bakers trade bread recipes on a knead-to-know basis.

25. Santa's helpers are subordinate clauses.

26. Acupuncture is a jab well done.

27. Marathon runners with bad footwear suffer the agony of the feet.

28. A bicycle can't stand alone; it is two tired.

13) CHILDREN

Heaven

A teacher is testing the children in her Sunday school class to see if they understood the concept of getting to Heaven. She asked them, "If I sold my house and my car, had a big garage sale and gave all my money to the church, would that get me into Heaven?" "NO!" the children answer. "If I clean the church every day, mow the yard, and keep everything neat and tidy, would that get me into Heaven?" Again, the answer is, "NO!" By now the teacher is starting to smile. Hey, this was fun! "Well, then, if I am kind to animals and give candy to all the children, and love my husband, would that get me into Heaven?" She asks them again. Again, they all answer, "NO!" The teacher is just bursting with pride for them. Well, she continues, "Then how can I get into Heaven?" A five-year-old boy shouts out, "YOU GOTTA BE DEAD."

Letter to Mom

A mother passing by her daughter's bedroom is astonished to see the bed was nicely made and everything was picked up. Then she sees an envelope propped up prominently on the center of the bed. It is addressed: "Mom." With the worst premonition, she opens the envelope and reads the letter with trembling hands:

"Dear Mom,

It is with great regret and sorrow that I'm writing you. I had to elope with my new boyfriend because I wanted to avoid a scene with Dad and you. I've been finding real passion with Ali and he is so nice – even with all his piercing, tattoos, beard, and his motorcycle clothes. But it's not only the passion, Mom, I'm pregnant and Ali said that we will be very happy. He already owns a trailer in the woods and has a stack of firewood for the whole winter. He wants to have many more children with me and that's now one of my dreams too. Ali taught me that marijuana doesn't really hurt anyone and we'll be growing it for us and trading it with his friends for all the cocaine and ecstasy we want. In the meantime, we'll pray that science will find a cure for AIDS so Ali can get better; he sure deserves it!! Don't

*worry Mom, I'm fifteen years old now and I know how
to take care of myself. Some day I'm sure we'll be back
to visit so you can get to know your grandchildren.*

Your daughter,

Judith

*PS: Mom, none of the above is true. I'm over at the
neighbor's house. I just wanted to remind you that there
are worse things in life than my report card which is in
my desk drawer. I love you! Call when it is safe for me
to come home."*

Reply to Judith

(sent by her father to the neighbors')

"Dear Judith,

*We received your letter. You mom only made it half
way through it and had a massive heart attack and
died. I only made it three quarters of the way through
and am heading to the Golden Gate bridge to throw
myself off at this moment.*

Your Father who loves you.

*PS: None of the above is true. . . Remember that
during your three-month grounding with no phone
calls. Things could be worse."*

Things I've Learned from my Children

1. A king size waterbed holds enough water to fill a 2000
    sq.ft. (609.6 sqm) house four inches (10.16 cm) deep.

2. If you spray hair spray on dust bunnies and run over them with Roller blades, they can ignite.

3. A three-year old's voice is louder than two hundred adults in a crowded restaurant.

4. If you hook a dog leash over a ceiling fan, the motor is not strong enough to rotate a forty-two-pound (nineteen-kilo) boy wearing Batman underwear and a Superman cape. It is strong enough, however, if tied to a paint can, to spread paint on all four walls of a twenty-by-twenty foot (six-by-six meter) room.

5. You should not throw baseballs up when the ceiling fan is on. When using a ceiling fan as a bat, you have to throw the ball up a few times before you get a hit. A ceiling fan can hit a baseball a long way.

6. The glass in windows (even double-pane) doesn't stop a baseball hit by a ceiling fan.

7. When you hear the toilet flush and the words "uh oh", it's already too late.

8. Brake fluid mixed with Clorox®[83] makes smoke, and lots of it.

9. A six-year old can start a fire with a flint rock even though a thirty-six year old man says they can only do it in the movies.

10. Certain Lego's®[84] will pass through the digestive tract of a four-year old.

11. Play Dough®[85] and microwave should not be used in the same sentence.

12. Super Glue®[86] is forever.

13.   No matter how much Jell-O® you put in a swimming pool you still can't walk on water.

14.   Pool filters do not like Jell-O®.

15.   VCRs[87] do not eject peanut-butter-and-jelly sandwiches even though TV commercials show they do.

16.   Garbage bags do not make good parachutes.

17.   Marbles in gas tanks make lots of noise when driving.

18.   Always look in the oven before you turn it on; plastic toys do not like ovens.

19.   The spin cycle on the washing machine does not make earthworms dizzy.

20.   It will, however, make cats dizzy.

21.   Cats throw up twice their body weight when dizzy.

22.   The mind of a six-year old is wonderful. First grade-true story. One day the first-grade teacher is reading the story of the Three Little Pigs to her class. She comes to the part of the story where the first pig is trying to accumulate the building materials for his home. She reads, ."..And so the pig went up to the man with the wheelbarrow full of straw and said, 'Pardon me sir, but may I have some of that straw to build my house?'" The teacher pauses, then asks the class, ."..And what do you think that man said?" One little boy raises his hand and says, "I think he said 'Holy crap! A talking pig!'"

Seven Reasons not to Mess with Children.

(Allegedly Genuine Quotes – Authenticity Unverified)

Reason 1

A little girl is talking to her teacher about whales. The teacher says it was physically impossible for a whale to swallow a human because even though it is a very large mammal its throat is very small. The little girl states that Jonah was swallowed by a whale. Irritated, the teacher reiterates that a whale could not swallow a human; it is physically impossible. The little girl says, "When I get to Heaven I will ask Jonah." The teacher asks, "What if Jonah went to Hell?" The little girl replies, "Then you ask him."

Reason 2

A kindergarten teacher is observing her classroom of children while they were drawing. She occasionally walks around to see each child's work. As she gets to one little girl who is working diligently, she asks what the drawing is. The girl replies, "I'm drawing God." The teacher pauses and says, "But no one knows what God looks like." Without missing a beat, or looking up from her drawing, the girl replies, "They will in a minute."

Reason 3

A Sunday school teacher is discussing the Ten Commandments with her five and six-year olds. After explaining the commandment to "honor thy Father and thy Mother", she asks, "Is there a commandment that teaches us how to treat our brothers and sisters?" One little boy (the oldest of a family) answers, "Thou shall not kill."

Reason 4

One day a little girl is sitting and watching her mother do the dishes at the kitchen sink. She suddenly notices that her mother has several strands of white hair sticking out in contrast on her brunette head. She looks at her mother and inquisitively asks, "Why are some of your hairs white, Mom?" Her mother replies, "Well, every time that you do something wrong and make me cry or unhappy, one of my hairs turns white." The little girl thought about this revelation for a while and then says, "Momma, that's why ALL of grandma's hairs are white?"

Reason 5

The children have all been photographed, and the teacher is trying to persuade them each to buy a copy of the group picture. "Just think how nice it will be to look at it when you are all grown up and say, 'There's Jennifer, she's a lawyer,' or 'That's Michael, He's a doctor.' A small voice at the back of the room rings out, "And there's the teacher, she's dead."

Reason 6

A teacher is giving a lesson on the circulation of the blood. Trying to make the matter clearer, she says, "Now, class, if I stand on my head, the blood, as you know, will run into it, and I will turn red in the face." "Yes," the class says. "Then why is it that while I am standing upright in the ordinary position the blood doesn't run into my feet?" A little fellow shouts, "Cause your feet ain't empty."

Reason 7

The children are lined up in the cafeteria of a Catholic elementary school for lunch. At the head of the table is a large pile of apples. The nun made a note, and posted on the apple tray: "Take only ONE. God is watching." Moving further along the lunch line, at the other end of the table is a large pile of chocolate chip cookies. A child had written a note, "Take all you want. God is watching the apples."

Why We Love Children

(Allegedly Genuine Quotes – Authenticity Unverified)

A kindergarten pupil tells his teacher he's found a cat, but it was dead. "How do you know that the cat was dead?" she asks her pupil. "Because I pissed in its ear and it didn't move," answers the child innocently. "You did WHAT?!?" the teacher exclaims in surprise. "You know," explains the boy, "I leaned over and went 'Pssst!' and it didn't move."

A small boy is sent to bed by his father. Five minutes later... "Da-ad...." "What?" "I'm thirsty. Can you bring drink of water?" "No, you had your chance. Lights out." Five minutes later: "Da-aaaad…" "WHAT?" "I'm THIRSTY. Can I have a drink of water??" "I told you NO! If you ask again, I'll have to spank you!!" Five minutes later…… "Daaaa-aaaad...." "WHAT!" "When you come in to spank me, can you bring a drink of water?"

An exasperated mother, whose son is always getting into mischief, finally asks him, "How do you expect to get into

Heaven?" The boy thinks it over and says, "Well, I'll run in and out and in and out and keep slamming the door until St. Peter says, 'For Heaven's sake, Dylan, come in or stay out'!"

One summer evening during a violent thunderstorm a mother is tucking her son into bed. She is about to turn off the light when he asks with a tremor in his voice, "Mommy, will you sleep with me tonight?" The mother smiles and gives him a reassuring hug. "I can't dear," she says. "I have to sleep in Daddy's room." A long silence is broken at last by his shaky little voice: "The big sissy."

It is that time, during the Sunday morning service, for the children's sermon. All the children are invited to come forward. One little girl is wearing a particularly pretty dress and, as she sits down, the pastor leans over and says, "That is a very pretty dress. Is it your Easter Dress?" The little girl replies, directly into the pastor's clip-on microphone, "Yes and my Mom says it's a bitch to iron."

A three-year old boy watches his mother pregnant with her third child while she is just getting ready to get into the shower. He says, "Mommy, you are getting fat!" The mother replies, "Yes, honey, remember Mommy has a baby growing in her tummy." "I know," he replies, "but what's growing in your butt?"

A little boy is doing his math homework. He says to himself, "Two plus five, that son of a bitch is seven. Three plus six, that son of a bitch is nine...." His mother hears what he is saying and gasps, "What are you doing?" The little boy answers, "I'm doing my math homework, Mom." "And this is how your teacher taught you to do it?" the mother asks. "Yes," he answers. Infuriated, the mother asks the teacher the next day, "What are you teaching my son in math?" The teacher replies, "Right now, we are learning addition." The mother asks, "And are you teaching them to say two plus two, that son of a bitch is four?" After the teacher stopped laughing, she answers, "What I taught them was, two plus two, THE SUM OF WHICH, is four."

A certain little girl, when asked her name, would reply, "I'm Mr. Sugarbrown's daughter." Her mother told her this was wrong, she must say, "I'm Jane Sugarbrown." The Vicar speaks to her in Sunday School, and asks, "Aren't you Mr. Sugarbrown's daughter?" She replies, "I thought I was, but mother says I'm not."

A little girl asks her mother, "Can I go outside and play with the boys?" Her mother replies, "No, you can't play with the boys, they're too rough." The little girl thinks about it for a few moments and asks, "If I can find a smooth one, can I play with him?"

A little girl goes to the barber shop with her father she stands next to the barber chair, while her dad gets his hair cut, eating a snack cake. The barber says to her, "Sweetheart, you're going to get hair on your Twinkie." She says, "Yes, I know, and I'm going to get boobs too."

What Does Love Mean?

(Allegedly Genuine Quotes – Authenticity Unverified)

A group of professional people posed this question to a group of four to eight-year olds, "What does love mean?" The answers they got were broader and deeper than anyone could have imagined.

"When my grandmother got arthritis, she couldn't bend over and paint her toenails anymore. So my grandfather does it for her all the time, even when his hands got arthritis too. That's love." (Rebecca – age 8)

"When someone loves you, the way they say your name is different. You just know that your name is safe in their mouth." (Billy – age 4)

"Love is when a girl puts on perfume and a boy puts on shaving cologne and they go out and smell each other." (Karl – age 5)

"Love is when you go out to eat and give somebody most of your French fries without making them give you any of theirs." (Chrissy – age 6)

"Love is what makes you smile when you're tired." (Terri – age 4)

"Love is when my Mommy makes coffee for my Daddy and she takes a sip before giving it to him, to make sure the taste is OK." (Danny – age 7)

"Love is when you kiss all the time. Then when you get tired of kissing, you still want to be together and you talk more. My Mommy and Daddy are like that. They look gross when they kiss." (Emily – age 8)

"Love is what's in the room with you at Christmas if you stop opening presents and listen." (Bobby – age 7)

"If you want to learn to love better, you should start with a friend who you hate." (Nikka – age 6)

"Love is when you tell a guy you like his shirt, then he wears it everyday." (Noelle – age 7)

"Love is like a little old woman and a little old man who are still friends even after they know each other so well." (Tommy – age 6)

"During my piano recital, I was on a stage and I was scared. I looked at all the people watching me and saw my daddy waving and smiling. He was the only one doing that. I wasn't scared anymore." (Cindy – age 8)

"My Mommy loves me more than anybody. You don't see anyone else kissing me to sleep at night." (Clare – age 6)

"Love is when Mommy gives Daddy the best piece of chicken." (Elaine-age 5)

"Love is when Mommy sees Daddy smelly and sweaty and still says he is handsomer than Robert Redford." (Chris – age 7)

"Love is when your puppy licks your face even after you left him alone all day." (Mary Ann – age 4)

"I know my older sister loves me because she gives me all her old clothes and has to go out and buy new ones." (Lauren – age 4)

"When you love somebody, your eyelashes go up and down and little stars come out of you." (Karen – age 7)

"Love is when Mommy sees Daddy on the toilet and she doesn't think it's gross." (Mark – age 6)

"You really shouldn't say 'I love you' unless you mean it. But if you mean it, you should say it a lot. People forget." (Jessica – age 8)

And the final one – Author and lecturer Leo Buscaglia once talked about a contest he was asked to judge. The purpose of the contest was to find the most caring child. The winner was a four-year old child whose next-door neighbor was an elderly gentleman who had recently lost his wife. Upon seeing the man cry, the little boy went into the old gentleman's yard, climbed onto his lap, and just sat there. When his mother asked what he had said to the neighbor, the little boy said, "Nothing, I just helped him cry."

Kids are Quick

(Allegedly Genuine Quotes – Authenticity Unverified)
TEACHER: "Maria, go to the map and find North America."
MARIA: "Here it is."

TEACHER: "Correct. Now class, who discovered America?"

CLASS: "Maria!"

TEACHER: "John, why are you doing your math multiplication on the floor?"

JOHN: "You told me to do it without using tables."

TEACHER: "Glenn, how do you spell 'crocodile?'"

GLENN: "K-R-O-K-O-D-I-A-L"

TEACHER: "No, that's wrong."

GLENN: "Maybe it is wrong, but you asked me how I spell it."

TEACHER: "Donald, what is the chemical formula for water?"

DONALD: "H I J K L M N O."

TEACHER: "What are you talking about?"

DONALD: "Yesterday you said it's H to O."

TEACHER: "Winnie, name one important thing we have today that we didn't have ten years ago."

WINNIE: "Me!"

TEACHER: "Glen, why do you always get so dirty?"

GLEN: "Well, I'm a lot closer to the ground than you are."

TEACHER: "George Washington not only chopped down his father's cherry tree, but also admitted it. Now, Louie, do you know why his father didn't punish him?"

LOUIS: "Because George still had the axe in his hand."

TEACHER: "Now, Simon, tell me frankly, do you say prayers before eating?"

SIMON: "No sir, I don't have to, my Mom is a good cook."

TEACHER: "Clyde, your composition on 'My Dog' is exactly the same as your brother's. Did you copy his?"

CLYDE: "No, teacher, it's the same dog."

TEACHER: "Mark, what do you call a person who keeps on talking when people are no longer interested?"

MARK: "A teacher."

Little Leroy

Little Leroy comes into the kitchen where his mother is making dinner. His birthday is coming up and he thinks this is a good time to tell his mother what he wants. "Mom, I want a bike for my birthday." Little Leroy was a bit of a troublemaker. He had got into trouble at school and at home. Leroy's mother asks him if he thinks he deserved to get a bike for his birthday. "Of course", he says. Leroy's mother, being a Christian woman, wants him to reflect on his behavior over the last year. "Go to your room, Leroy, and think about how you have behaved this year. Then write a letter to God and tell him why you deserve a bike for your birthday." Little Leroy stomps up the steps to his room and sits down to write God a letter.

Letter 1

"Dear God, I have been a very good boy this year and I would like a bike for my birthday. I want a red one. Your friend, Leroy."

Leroy knows that it is not true. He has not been a good boy this year, so he tears it up and starts over.

Letter 2

"Dear God, I have been an OK boy this year. I still would like a bike for my birthday. Leroy."

Leroy knows he cannot send this letter to God either. So, Leroy writes a third letter.

Letter 3

"Dear God, I know I haven't been a good boy this year. I am very sorry. I will be a good boy if you just send me a bike for my birthday. Please! Thank you, Leroy."

Leroy knows that it is not true. By now he is very upset. He goes downstairs and tells his mother that he needs to go to church. She thinks her plan has worked. "Just be home for dinner," she tells him. Leroy walks down the street to the church on the corner. He goes to the altar. Leroy looks around to see if anyone is looking as he bents down and picks up a statue of the Virgin Mary. He slips it up under his shirt and runs out the church going back home. He runs to his room and shuts the door. Leroy begins to write his letter to God.

Letter 4

"Dear God, I got your Mama. If you want to see her again, send the bike. Signed, You know who."

How Do You Decide Whom to Marry?

(Written by Kids – Authenticity Unverified)

You got to find somebody who likes the same stuff. Like, if you like sports, she should like it that you like sports, and she should keep the chips and dip coming.— *Alan, age 10*

No person really decides before they grow up who they're going to marry. God decides it all way before, and you get to find out later who you're stuck with.— *Kristen, age 10*

What is the Right Age to Get Married?

Twenty-three is the best age because you know the person FOREVER by then.— *Camille, age 10*

How Can a Stranger Tell if Two People are Married?

You might have to guess, based on whether they seem to be yelling at the same kids.— *Derrick, age 8*

What Do You Think Your Mom and Dad Have in Common?

Both don't want any more kids.— *Lori, age 8*

What Do Most People Do on a Date?

Dates are for having fun, and people should use them to get to know each other. Even boys have something to say if you listen long enough.— *Lynnette, age 8*

On the first date, they just tell each other lies and that usually gets them interested enough to go for a second date.— *Martin, age 10*

What Would You Do on a First Date that Was Turning Sour?

I'd run home and play dead. The next day I would call all the newspapers and make sure they wrote about me in all the dead columns.— *Craig, age 9*

When Is It Okay to Kiss Someone?

When they're rich.— *Pam, age 7*

The law says you have to be eighteen, so I wouldn't want to mess with that.—*Curt, age 7*

The rule goes like this: if you kiss someone, then you should marry them and have kids with them. It's the right thing to do.— *Howard, age 8*

Is It Better to Be Single or Married?

It's better for girls to be single but not for boys. Boys need someone to clean up after them.— *Anita, age 9*

How Would the World Be Different if People Didn't Get Married?

There sure would be a lot of kids to explain, wouldn't there? — *Kelvin, age 8*

How Would You Make a Marriage Work?

Tell your wife that she looks pretty, even if she looks like a truck.— *Ricky, age 10*

At the Bank

A mother takes her five-year old son with her to the bank on a busy lunchtime. They get behind a very fat woman wearing a business suit complete with pager. As they wait patiently, the little boy says loudly, "Gee, she's fat!" The mother bents down and whispers in the little boy's ear to be quiet. A couple of minutes pass by and the little boy spreads his hands as far as they would go and announces, "I'll bet her butt is this wide!" The fat woman turns around and glares at the little boy. The mother gives him a good telling off, and tells him to be quiet. After a brief lull, the large woman reaches the front of the line. Just then, her pager begins to emit a "Beep, beep, beep." The little boy yells out, "Run for your life, she's backing up!!"

14) HEAVEN, HELL AND CLERGY

Hell and Heat

The following is supposedly an actual question given on a University of Washington chemistry mid-term exam. The answer by one (anonymous) student was so "profound" that the professor shared it with colleagues, via the Internet, which is, of course, why we now have the pleasure of enjoying it as well.

Bonus Question: "Is Hell exothermic (gives off heat) or endothermic (absorbs heat)?"

Most of the students wrote proofs of their beliefs using Boyle's Law (gas cools when it expands and heats when it is compressed or some variant). One student, however, wrote the following answer.

"First, we need to know how the mass of Hell is changing in time. So we need to know the rate at which souls are moving into Hell and the rate at which they are leaving. I think that we can safely assume that once a soul gets to Hell, it will not leave. Therefore, no souls are leaving. As for how many souls are entering Hell, let's look at the different religions that exist in the world today. Most of these religions state that if you are not a member of their religion, you will go to Hell. Since there is more than one of these religions and since people do not belong to more than one religion, we can project that all souls go to Hell. With birth and death rates as they are, we can expect the number of souls in Hell to increase exponentially. Now, we look at the rate of change of the volume in Hell because Boyle's Law states that in order for the temperature and pressure in Hell to stay the same, the volume of Hell has to expand proportionately as souls are added. This gives two possibilities:

1. If Hell is expanding at a slower rate than the rate at which souls enter Hell, then the temperature and pressure in Hell will increase until all Hell breaks loose.

2. If Hell is expanding at a rate faster than the increase of souls in Hell, then the temperature and pressure will drop until Hell freezes over.

So which is it? If we accept the postulate given to me by Teresa during my Freshman year that, "it will be a cold day in Hell before I sleep with you", and take into account the fact that I slept with her last night, then number 2 must be true, and thus I am sure that Hell is exothermic and has already frozen over.

The corollary of this theory is that since Hell has frozen over, it follows that it is not accepting any more souls and is therefore, extinct. . . leaving only Heaven, thereby proving the existence of a divine being, which explains why, last night, Teresa kept shouting, 'Oh my God.'"

This student received the only 'A'.

Hell Again

One day a guy dies and finds himself in Hell. As he is wallowing in despair, he has his first meeting with a demon. The demon asks, "Why so glum?" The guy responds, "What do you think? I'm in Hell!" "Hell's not so bad," the demon says. "We actually have a lot of fun down here. Are you a drinking man?" "Sure," the man says, "I love to drink." "Well, you're gonna love Mondays then. On Mondays all we do is drink. Whiskey, tequila, Guinness®, wine coolers, Diet Tab® and Fresca®. We drink till we throw up and then we drink some more!" The guy is astounded. "Damn, that sounds great." "Are you a smoker?" the demon asks. "You better believe it!" "You're gonna love Tuesdays. We get the finest cigars from all over the world and smoke our lungs out! If you get cancer, no biggie. You're already dead, remember?" "Wow, the guy says, "that's awesome!" The demon continues, "I bet you like to gamble." "Why yes, as a matter of fact I do." "Wednesdays you can gamble all you want. Craps, blackjack, roulette, poker, slots, whatever. If you go bankrupt, well, you're dead anyhow. Are you into drugs?" The guy says, "Are you kidding? I love drugs! You don't mean..." "That's right! Thursday is drug day. Help yourself to a great big bowl of crack, or smack. Smoke a doobie the size of a submarine. You can do all the drugs you want, you're dead, who cares!" "Wow," the guy says, starting to feel better about his situation, "I never realized Hell was such a cool place!" The demon asks, "Are you gay?" "No." "Ooooh, you're gonna hate Fridays!"

Parrots

A lady goes to her priest one day and tells him, "Father, I have a problem. I have two female parrots, but they only know how to say one thing." "What do they say?" the priest asks. "They say, 'Hi, we're hookers! Do you want to have some fun?'" "That's obscene!" the priest exclaims; then he thinks for a moment. "You know, I have two male talking parrots that I have taught to pray and read the Bible. Bring your two parrots over to my house, and we'll put them in the cage with Francis and Job. My parrots can teach your parrots to praise and worship, and your parrots are sure to stop saying that phrase in no time." "Thank you," the woman says, "this may be the solution." The next day, she brings her female parrots to the priest's house. As he ushers her in, she sees that his two male parrots are inside their cage holding rosary beads and praying. Impressed, she walks over and places her parrots in with them. After a few minutes, the female parrots cry out in unison, "Hi, we're hookers! Do you want to have some fun?" There is stunned silence. Shocked, one male parrot looks over at the other male parrot and exclaims, "Put the beads away, Frank. Our prayers have been answered!"

Warning

A burglar breaks into a house one night. He shines his flashlight around, looking for valuables, and when he picks up a CD player to place in his sack, a strange, disembodied voice echoes from the dark, saying, "Jesus is watching you." He nearly jumps out of his skin, clicks his flashlight off, and freezes. When he hears nothing more after a bit, he shakes his head, promises himself a vacation after the next big score, then clicks the light on and begins searching for more valuables. Just as he pulls the stereo out so he can disconnect the wires, clear as a bell he hears again, "Jesus is watching you." Freaked out, he shines his light around frantically, looking for the source of the voice. Finally, in the corner of the room, his flashlight beam comes to rest on a parrot! "Did you say that?" he hisses at the parrot. "Yep," the parrot confesses, then squawks, "I'm just trying to warn you." The burglar relaxes. "Warn me, huh? Who in the world are you?" "I'm Moses," replies the bird. "Moses?" the burglar laughs. "What kind of people would name their bird Moses?" "The kind of people who would name their Rottweiler Jesus."

Moses

While going through an airport during one of his many trips, President Bush encounters a man with long grey hair, wearing a white robe and sandals, holding a staff. President Bush goes up to the man and says, "Has anyone told you that you look like Moses?" The man doesn't answer. He just keeps staring straight ahead. The president says, "Moses!" in a loud voice. The man just stares ahead, never acknowledging the President. The President pulls a Secret Service agent aside and, pointing to the robed man, asks him, "Am I crazy or does that man not look like Moses to you?" The Secret Service agent looks at the man and agrees. "Well," says the President, "every time I say his name, he ignores me and stares straight ahead, refusing to speak. Watch!" Again the President yells, "Moses!" and again the man ignores him. The Secret Service agent goes up to the man in the white robe and whispers, "You look just like Moses. Are you Moses?" The man leans over and whispers back, "Yes, I am Moses. However, the last time I talked to a bush, I spent forty years wandering in the desert and ended up leading my people to the only spot in the entire Middle East where there is no oil."

Hawaii

Two priests decide to go to Hawaii on vacation. They are determined to make this a real vacation by not wearing anything that would identify them as clergy. As soon as the plane lands they head for a store and buy some really outrageous shorts, shirts, sandals, sunglasses, etc. The next morning they go to the beach dressed in their "tourist" garb. They are sitting on beach chairs, enjoying a drink, the sunshine and the scenery when a "drop-dead-gorgeous" topless blonde in a thong bikini comes walking straight towards them. They couldn't help but stare. As the blonde passes them she smiles and said, "Good Morning, Father. Good Morning, Father," nodding and addressing each of them individually; then she passes on by. They are both stunned.

How in the world does she know they are priests? So, the next day, they go back to the store and buy even more outrageous outfits. These are so loud you could hear them before you even saw them. Once again, in their new attire, they settle on the beach in their chairs to enjoy the sunshine. After a while, the same gorgeous topless blonde, wearing a string bikini, taking her sweet time, comes walking toward them. Again she nods at each of them, says, "Good morning, Father. Good morning, Father," and starts to walk away. One of the priests can't stand it any longer and says, "Just a minute, young lady." "Yes, Father?" she said. "We are priests and proud of it, but I have to know, how in the world did you know we are priests, dressed as we are?" "Father, it's me, Sister Katherine," she replies.

Convent Fire

Several elderly nuns are in their second floor convent one night when a fire breaks out. They take their habits off, tie them together to make a rope, and climb out the window. After they are safely on the ground and out of the building, a news reporter comes over to one of the nuns and says to her, "Weren't you afraid that the habits could have ripped or broken since they are old?" The nun replies, "Nah, don't you know old habits are hard to break!!"

Santa Claus

"Oh Christmas Tree, Oh Christmas Tree......." Four of Santa's elves are sick, and the trainee elves did not produce the toys as fast as the regular ones, so Santa Claus is beginning to feel the pressure of being behind schedule. Then Mrs. Claus tells Santa that her Mom is coming to visit. This stresses Santa even more. When he goes to harness the reindeer, he finds that three of them are about to give birth and two have jumped the fence and are out, heaven knows where. More stress.. . . then when he begins to load the sleigh one of the boards cracks, and the toy bag falls to the ground and scatters the toys. So, frustrated, Santa goes into the house for a cup of apple cider and a shot of rum. When he goes to the cupboard, he discovers that the elves have hidden the liquor, and there is nothing to drink. In his frustration, he accidentally drops the cider pot, and it breaks into hundreds of little pieces all over the kitchen floor. He goes to get the broom and finds that mice have eaten the straw end of the broom. Just then the doorbell rings, and irritable Santa trudges to the door. He opens the door, and there is a little angel with a great big Christmas tree. The angel says, very cheerfully, "Merry Christmas, Santa. Isn't it a lovely day? I have a beautiful tree for you. Where would you like me to stick it?" ...and so began the tradition of the little angel on top of the Christmas tree.

Marketing

A minister concludes that his church is getting into serious financial troubles. Coincidentally, by chance, while checking the church storeroom, he discovers several cartons of new bibles that have never been opened and distributed. So at his Sunday sermon, he asks for three volunteers from the congregation who would be willing to sell the bibles door-to-door for ten dollars each to raise the desperately needed money for the church. Peter, Paul and Louie all raise their hands to volunteer for the task. The reverend knows that Peter and Paul earn their living as salesmen and are likely capable of selling some bibles but he has serious doubts about Louie, a little local farmer, who has always tended to keep to himself because he was embarrassed by his speech impediment. Poor little Louis stutter very badly. But, not wanting to discourage poor Louis, the reverend decides to let him try anyway. He sends the three of them away with the back seat of their cars stacked with bibles and asks them to meet with him and report the results of their door-to-door selling efforts the following Sunday. Anxious to find out how successful they were, the reverend immediately asks Peter, "Well, Peter, how did you make out selling our bibles last week?" Proudly handing the reverend an envelope, Peter replies, "Father, using my sales prowess, I was able to sell twenty bibles, and here's the two hundred dollars I collected on behalf of the church." "Fine job, Peter!" The reverend says, vigorously shaking his hand. "You are indeed a fine salesman and the church is indebted to you." Turning to Paul, he asks, "And Paul, how many bibles did you manage to sell for the church last week?" Paul, smiling and sticking out his chest, confidently replies, "Reverend, I am a professional salesman and was happy to give the church the benefit of my sales expertise. Last week I sold twenty-eight bibles on behalf of the church, and here's two hundred and eighty dollars I collected." The reverend responds, "That's absolutely splendid, Paul. You are truly a professional salesman and the church is also indebted to you." Apprehensively, the reverend turns to little Louie and said, "And Louie, did you manage to sell any bibles last week?" Louie silently offers the reverend a large envelope. The reverend opens it and counts the contents. "What is this?" the reverend exclaims. "Louie, there's three thousand two hundred dollards in here! Are you suggesting that you sold three hundred and twenty bibles for the church, door to door, in just one week?" Louie just nods. "That's impossible!" both Peter and Paul say in unison. "We are professional salesmen, yet you claim to have sold ten times as many bibles as we could." "Yes, this does seem unlikely," the reverend agrees. "I think you'd better explain how you managed to accomplish this, Louie." Louie shrugs. "I-I-I- rc-rc-really do-do-don't kn-kn-know f-f-f-for sh-sh-sh-sure," he stammers. Impatiently, Peter interrupts. "For crying out loud, Louie, just tell us what you said to them when they answered the door!" "A-a-a-all I-I-I s-s-said wa-wa-was," Louis replies, "W-w-w-w-would y-y-y-you l-l-l-l-like t-t-to b-b-b-buy th-th-th-this b-b-b-b-bible f-f-for t-t-ten b-b-b-bucks —o-o-o-or— wo-wo-would yo-you j-j-j-just l-like m-m-me t-t-to st-st-stand h-h-here and r-r-r-r-read it t-to y-y-you?"

Worry

There are only two things to worry about: either you are well or you are sick. But if you are well, there is nothing to worry about. If you are sick, there are only two things to worry about: either you will get well or you will die. But if you get well, there is nothing to worry about. If you die, there are only two things to worry about: either you go to Heaven or you go to Hell.

But if you go to Heaven, there is nothing to worry about. If you go to Hell, you'll be so damn busy shaking hands with friends that you won't have time to worry.

Nuns

Mother Superior calls all the nuns together and says to them, "I must tell you all something. We have a case of gonorrhea in the convent." "Thank Goodness," said an elderly nun at the back. "I'm so tired of chardonnay."

15) DOGS

Sniffer

A man gets into his seat on an airplane, which is about to take off, when another man with a Labrador Retriever occupies the two empty seats beside him. The Lab is situated in the middle, and the first man is looking quizzically at the dog when the second man explains that they work for the airline. The airline rep says, "Don't mind Sniffer. He's a sniffing dog, the best there is. I'll show you once we get airborne when I put him to work." The plane takes off and levels out when the handler says to the first man, "Watch this." He tells the dog, "Sniffer, search." Sniffer jumps down, walks along the aisle, and sits next to a woman for a few seconds. It then returns to its seat and puts one paw on the handler's arm. He says, "Good boy." The airline rep turns to the first man and says, "That woman is in possession of marijuana, so I'm making a note of this and her seat number for the police who will apprehend her upon arrival." "Fantastic!" replies the first man. Once again, he sends Sniffer to search the aisles. The Lab sniffs about, sits down beside a man for a few seconds, returns to its seat, and places two paws on the handler's arm. The airline rep says, "That man is carrying cocaine, so, again, I'm making a note of this and the seat number." "I like it!" says the first man. A third time, the rep sends Sniffer to search the aisles. Sniffer goes up and down the plane and, after a while, sits down next to someone. He then comes racing back, jumps up onto his seat, and poops all over the place. The first man is really grossed out by this behavior from a supposedly well-trained sniffing dog and asks, "What's going on?" The handler nervously replies, "He just found a bomb!"

Vet

A man takes his Rotteweiller to the vet. "My dog's cross-eyed, is there anything you can do for him?" "Well," says the vet, "let's have a look at him." So he picks the dog up and examines his eyes, then checks his teeth. Finally, he says, "I'm going to have to put him down." "What? Because he's cross-eyed?" "No, because he's really heavy."

Man's Best Friend

A man and his dog are walking along a road. The man is enjoying the scenery, when it suddenly occurs to him that he is dead. He remembers dying, and that the dog walking beside him has been dead for years. He wonders where the road is leading them. After a while, they come to a high, white stone wall along one side of the road. It looks like fine marble. At the top of a long hill, it is broken by a tall arch that glows in the sunlight. When he is standing before it he sees a magnificent gate in the arch that looks like Mother of Pearl, and the street that leads to the gate looks like pure gold. He and the dog walk toward the gate, and as he gets closer, he sees a man at a desk to one side. When he is close enough, he calls out, "Excuse me, where are we?" "This is Heaven, sir," the man answers. "Wow! Would you happen to have some water?" the man asked. "Of course, Sir. Come right in, and I'll have some ice water brought right up." The man gestures, and the gate begins to open. "Can my friend," gesturing toward his dog, "come in, too?" the traveler asks. "I'm sorry, sir, but we don't accept pets." The man thinks a moment and then turns back toward the road and continues the way he has been going with his dog. After another long walk, and at the top of another long hill, he comes to a dirt road which leads through a farm gate that looks as if it had never been closed. There is no fence. As he approaches the gate, he sees a man inside, leaning against a tree and reading a book. "Excuse me!" he calls to the reader. "Do you have any water?" "Yeah, sure, there's a pump over there, come on in." "How about my friend here?" the traveler gestures to the dog. "There should be a bowl by the pump." They go through the gate, and sure enough, there is an old-fashioned hand pump with a bowl beside it. The traveler fills the bowl and takes a long drink himself, then he gives some to the dog. When they are full, he and the dog walk back toward the man who is standing by the tree. "What do you call this place?" the traveler asks. "This is Heaven," he answers. "Well, that's confusing," the traveler says. "The man down the road said that was Heaven, too." "Oh, you mean the place with the gold street and pearly gates? Nope. That's Hell." "Doesn't it make you mad for them to use your name like that?" "No, we're just happy that they screen out the folks who would leave their best friends behind."

Dog Philosophy

(Author of Compilation Anonymous)
"The reason a dog has so many friends is that he wags his tail instead of his tongue."
(Anonymous)

"Don't accept your dog's admiration as conclusive evidence that you are wonderful."
(Ann Landers)

"If there are no dogs in Heaven, then when I die I want to go where they went."
(Will Rogers)

"There is no psychiatrist in the world like a puppy licking your face."
(Ben Williams)

"A dog is the only thing on Earth that loves you more than he loves himself."
(*Josh Billings*)

"The average dog is a nicer person than the average person."
(*Andy Rooney*)

"We give dogs time we can spare, space we can spare and love we can spare. And in return, dogs give us their all. It's the best deal Man has ever made."
(*M. Acklam*)

"Dogs love their friends and bite their enemies, quite unlike people, who are incapable of pure love and always have to mix love and hate."
(*Sigmund Freud*)

"I wonder if other dogs think poodles are members of a weird religious cult."
(*Rita Rudner*)

"A dog teaches a boy fidelity, perseverance, and to turn around three times before lying down."
(*Robert Benchley*)

"Anybody who doesn't know what soap tastes like never washed a dog."
(*Franklin P. Jones*)

"If I have any beliefs about immortality, it is that certain dogs I have known will go to Heaven, and very, very few persons."
(James Thurber)

"If your dog is fat, you aren't getting enough exercise."
(Unknown)

"My dog is worried about the economy because Alpo® is up to three dollars a can. That's almost twenty-one dollars in dog money."
(Joe Weinstein)

"Ever consider what our dogs must think of us? I mean, here we come back from a grocery store with the most amazing haul, chicken, pork, half a cow. They must think we're the greatest hunters on earth!"
(Anne Tyler)

"Women and cats will do as they please, and men and dogs should relax and get used to the idea."
(Robert A. Heinlein)

"If you pick up a starving dog and make him prosperous, he will not bite you; that is the principal difference between a dog and a man.
(Mark Twain)

"You can say any foolish thing to a dog, and the dog will give
you a look that says, 'Wow, you're right! I never would've
thought of that!'"

(Dave Barry)

"Dogs are not our whole life, but they make our lives whole."

(Roger Caras)

"If you think dogs can't count, try putting three dog biscuits in
your pocket and then give him only two of them."

(Phil Pastoret)

"My goal in life is to be as good of a person my dog already
thinks I am."

(Unknown)

16) COMPUTERS

Computer Virus Warning

There is a dangerous virus being passed electronically, oral-
ly and by hand. This virus is called Worm-Overload-
Recreational-Killer (WORK). If you receive WORK from any of your
colleagues, your boss or anyone else via any means DO NOT
TOUCH IT. This virus will wipe out your private life completely.
If you should come into contact with WORK put your jacket on
and take two good friends to the nearest bar. Purchase the antidote known as Work-Isolator-Neutralizer-Extractor (WINE). The
quickest acting WINE type is called Swift-Hitting-Infiltrator-

Remover-All-Zones (SHIRAZ)[88] but this is only available for those who can afford it, the next best equivalent is Cheapest-Available-System-Killer (CASK). Take the antidote repeatedly until WORK has been completely eliminated from your system. Forward this warning to five friends. If you do not have five friends you have already been infected and WORK is controlling your life. This virus is   DEADLY   (Destroys-Every-Available-Decent-Living-Youngster). After extensive testing it has been concluded that Best-Equivalent-Extractor-Remedy (BEER) may be substituted for WINE but may require a more generous application.

Why Computers Sometimes Crash!

(You need to read this one out loud)

If a packet hits a pocket on a socket on a port, and the bus is interrupted at a very last resort, and the access of the memory makes your floppy disk abort, then the socket packet pocket has an error to report. If your cursor finds a menu item followed by a dash, and the double-clicking icon puts your window in the trash, and your data is corrupted cause the index doesn't hash, then your situation's hopeless and your system's gonna crash! If the label on the cable on the table at your house, says the network is connected to the button on your mouse, but your packets want to tunnel to another protocol, that's repeatedly rejected by the printer down the hall. And your screen is all distorted by the side effects of gauss, so your icons in the window are as wavy as a souse; then you may as well reboot and go out with a bang, 'cuz sure as I'm a poet, the sucker's gonna hang. When the copy on your floppy's get-

ting sloppy in the disk, and the macro code instructions are causing unnecessary risk, then you'll have to flash the memory and you'll
want to RAM your ROM, and then quickly turn off the computer
and be sure to tell your Mom! Well, that certainly clears things up
for me. How about you? Thank you, Bill Gates, for bringing all
this into our lives.

Electronic Birds & Bees

Bobby asks, "Daddy, how was I born?" Dad answers, "Ah, my
son, I guess one day you will need to find out anyway! Well, you
see your Mom and I first got together in a chat room on MSN®. Then
I set up a date via e-mail with your Mom and we met at a cyber-
cafe. We sneaked into a secluded room, where your mother agreed
to a download from my hard drive. As soon as I was ready to up-
load, we discovered that neither one of us had used a firewall, and
since it was too late to hit the Delete button, nine months later a
blessed little Pop-Up appeared and said, 'you've got male!'"

Life Before the Computer

Memory was something you lost with age,
An application was for employment,
A program was a TV show,
A cursor used profanity,
A keyboard was a piano,
A web was a spider's home,
A virus was the flu,
A CD was a bank account,

A hard drive was a long trip on the road,

A mouse pad was where a mouse lived,

And if you had a 3-½ inch floppy...

You just hoped nobody ever found out.

Why Do You Forward Internet Jokes?

Sometimes, we wonder why friends keep forwarding jokes to us without writing a word, maybe this could explain: when you are very busy, but still want to keep in touch, guess what you do? You forward jokes. When you have nothing to say, but still want to keep contact, you forward jokes. When you have something to say, but don't know what, and don't know how, you forward jokes. And to let you know that you are still remembered, you are still important, you are still loved, you are still cared for, guess what you get? A forwarded joke. So, next time if you get a joke, don't think that you've been sent just another forwarded joke, but that you've been thought of today and your friend on the other end of your computer wanted to send you a smile.

17) MISCELLANEOUS

Quickies

Phone answering machine message – "If you want to buy marijuana, press the hash key..."

A guy walks into the psychiatrist wearing only Clingfilm®[89] for shorts. The shrink says, "Well, I can clearly see you're nuts."

I went to buy some camouflage trousers the other day but I couldn't find any.

I went to the butchers the other day and I bet him fifty bucks that he couldn't reach the meat off the top shelf. He said, "No, the steaks are too high."

My friend drowned in a bowl of muesli. A strong currant pulled him in.

A man comes round in hospital after a serious accident. He shouts, "Doctor, doctor, I can't feel my legs!" The doctor replies, "I know you can't, I've cut your arms off."

I went to a seafood disco last week. . . and pulled a muscle.

Two Eskimos sitting in a kayak are chilly. They light a fire in the craft, it sinks, proving once and for all that you can't have your kayak and heat it.

Our ice cream man was found lying on the floor of his van covered with hundreds and thousands. Police say that he topped himself.

Man goes to the doctor, with a strawberry growing out of his head. Doc says "I'll give you some cream to put on it."

"Doc I can't stop singing The Green, Green Grass of Home." "That sounds like 'Tom Jones syndrome'. "Is it common?"" "It's not unusual."

What do you call a fish with no eyes? A fsh.

So I was getting into my car, and this bloke says to me, "Can you give me a lift?" I said, "Sure, you look great, the world's your oyster, go for it."

Two fat blokes in a pub, one says to the other, "Your round." The other one says, "So are you, you fat bast**d!"

Police arrested two kids yesterday, one was drinking battery acid, and the other was eating fireworks. They charged one and let the other one off.

"You know, somebody actually complimented me on my driving today. They left a little note on the windscreen. It said, 'Parking Fine'. So that was nice."

A man walks into the doctors'; he says, "I've hurt my arm in several places." The doctor says, "Well don't go there anymore."

Mommy Bear

It's a sunny morning in the Big Forest and the Bear family is just waking up. Baby Bear goes downstairs and sits in his small chair at the table. He looks into his small bowl. It is empty! "Who's been eating my porridge?" he squeaks. Daddy Bear arrives at the table and sits in his big chair. He looks into his big bowl. It is also empty! "Who's been eating my porridge?" he roars. Mommy Bear puts her head through the serving hatch from the kitchen and yells, "For Pete's sake, how many times do we have to go through this? It was Mommy Bear who got up first. It was Mommy Bear who woke everybody else in the house up. It was Mommy Bear who unloaded the dishwasher from last night and put everything away. It was Mommy Bear who went out into the cold early morning air to fetch the newspaper. It was Mommy Bear who set the table. It was Mommy Bear who put the cat out, cleaned the litter box and filled the cat's water and food dish. And now that you've decided to come downstairs and grace me with your presence. . . Listen good because I'm only going to say this one more time. . . I haven't made the !@#$% porridge yet!!"

New Quick Ones

Two antennas meet on a roof, fall in love and get married. The ceremony wasn't much, but the reception was excellent.

■

Two hydrogen atoms walk into a bar. One says, "I've lost my electron." The other says, "Are you sure?" The first replies, "Yes. I'm positive…"

■

A jumper cable walks into a bar. The bartender says, "I'll serve you, but don't start anything."

■

Two peanuts walk into a bar, and one was a salted.

■

A sandwich walks into a bar. The bartender says, "Sorry we don't serve food in here."

■

A dyslexic man walks into a bra.

■

A man walks into a bar with a slab of asphalt under his arm and says, "A beer please, and one for the road."

■

Two cannibals are eating a clown. One says to the other, "Does this taste funny to you?"

■

Two cows standing next to each other in a field, Daisy says to Dolly, "I was artificially inseminated this morning." "I don't believe you," said Dolly. "It's true, no bull!" exclaimed Daisy.

■

An invisible man marries an invisible woman. The kids were nothing to look at either.

■

Two termites walk into a bar. One asks, "Is the bar tender here?"

Theory

Here is an interesting theory as food for thought: a herd of buffalo cannot move faster than its slowest buffalo. When the herd is chased by a predator, the weakest buffaloes remain the last and are killed first. This natural selection rule is a good thing for the herd as a whole since the general speed and the health of the group increase as its weakest members disappear. Similarly, the human brain cannot function faster than its slowest neurone. As every one knows, an excessive consumption of alcohol destroys neurons, but naturally the weakest neurons are attacked first.   Thus, a regular consumption of alcohol eliminates the weakest neurons, making the brain an ever faster and efficient machine. The result of this profound neurological study verifies and validates the causal relationship between week-end parties and the productivity of mathematicians, engineers, economists, lawyers, architects, etc. This is how, several years after graduating from the university and getting married, most professionals cannot sustain the productivity levels of freshly graduating students. Only the minority of those who persist in the strict diet of voracious consumption of alcohol can maintain their intellectual potential at their student years' level. For all these reasons, while our country is losing its intellectual potential, we cannot decently remain at home doing nothing: let's all go to the bar!

Fired

Peters learned that he is being fired, so he goes to see the head of human resources. "Since I've been with the firm for so long," he says, "I think I deserve at least a letter of recommendation." The human resources director agrees and says he will have the letter that next day. The following morning, Peters finds the letter on his desk. It reads, "Jonathan Peters worked for our company for eleven years. When he left us, we were very satisfied."

The Big Brain-Teaser

En Français Dans Le Texte

6

(Original French)

Ton corps raconte des histoires :
la chair est fable.

Je suis insomniaque. Au jour le jour,
la nuit me nuit.

Je suis Consul :
les expats m'épatent.

Les amoureux sont des forts en t'aime.

Mieux vaut une négociation interminable
qu'un accord minable.

Certains hommes politiques n'en ont rien à cirer du parquet.

Le chef d'un restaurant gastronomique accusé de corruption :
sa spécialité était le coq au pot-de-vin.

Scandale: après avoir conduit sa fille à l'autel,
un père conduit la demoiselle d'honneur à l'hôtel.

L'Eglise en déclin en France :
elle ne pèse plus très Lourdes.

Un repris de justice alphabétisé en prison,
une fois libre, vida son chargeur sur une porte :
il avait lu: « Tirez. »

Le même assomma un juge; il avait lu sur sa porte: « Frappez
fort. »

Les préoccupations liées à l'introduction de l'euro sont
monnaie courante.

Attentats à New York :
la « Grosse Pomme » a des pépins.

La prostituée est muette :
elle ne pipe mot.

Les lapins aussi ont droit au développement du râble.

Gratuité des transports en commun pour les handicapés :
les aveugles voyagent à l'œil.

Débat sur la laïcité : le gouvernement français lève le voile sur
sa politique,
mais chacun doit se faire une religion.

Autrefois, l'Occident avait peur de Mao.
Maintenant il a peur de Mahomet.

Économies budgétaires à l'ONU :
les soldats casquent bleu.

Pour lutter contre la canicule, le gouvernement n'a pas brûlé
les étapes.

Cette exposition de statues laissa le sculpteur de marbre.

Les clients d'un restaurant pris en otage :
ils ne sont pas sortis de l'auberge.

Un milliardaire avait une femme nymphomane :
il donnait des banquets ; elle se donnait sur des banquettes.

Le comble pour un journaliste :
travailler pour *Libération* et être capturé.

Emeutes en Australie :
les Aborigènes sortent de leur réserve.

Quand les paysans français sont mécontents, ils font du foin.
Mais le gouvernement n'en prend pas de la graine.

Les exclus de la société devraient créer une association « SOS
Ostracisme ».

Devise des intellectuels helvétiques :
« Je pense, donc je Suisse. »

Décès d'une personnalité suisse :
Genève est en berne.

Sur la Constitution européenne, les Français se disputent pour
un oui pour un non.

Un lion à une lionne :
« Nous sommes félins pour l'autre ».

Changements climatiques :
le temps était pluvieux ; il sera plus jeune.

J'ai des amis très différents :
un Namibien, un qui Népalais, un Genevois pas grand-chose et
un Ivoirien du tout.

Pourquoi parle-t-on de rentrée littéraire
quand de nouveaux livres sortent ?

Pour les habitants africains d'immeubles insalubres à Paris,
c'est la série noire.

On ne devrait pas parler de Ministère de la Défense
mais de Ministère de la Dépense.

Les jeunes banlieusards s'ennuient :
ils tournent comme des lions en cage d'escalier.

Des *rave parties* à la campagne :
de la techno pour les péquenots.

L'industrie du sexe en crise : le SM[90] frappé de plein fouet.

La crise franco-allemande éclata lorsque Jacques Chirac
engueula Merkel.

Dans de nombreux sports, les Blancs font pâle figure.

Les skieurs français ne gagnent plus de médailles :
ils ne savent plus ce qui est bien.

Moins de sportifs en France :
les marathoniens ne courent plus les rues.

Bien que je sois marseillais,
la pétanque me fout les boules.

En Europe, les mesures d'interdiction de fumer
ont fait un tabac.

Les arguments des partisans de la cigarette sont fumeux.

Ce qu'ont en commun bien des diplomates et des militaires :
le protocole, l'alcool et le cholestérol.

Nos grands-parents avaient le père Charles de Foucault.
Nos parents avaient Michel Foucault.
Il nous reste Jean-Pierre Foucault.[91]

Le message des candidats aux élections françaises :
« Elysée-moi, je ferai le reste. »

Exploitation de la peur et démagogie électorale :
« Demain, on rase les murs gratis. »

Manifestations contre la junte birmane :
le choc entre les bonzes et les mauvais.

Mise en garde aux investisseurs :
à Bakou les coûts sont bas, mais à Cuba, il y a des coups bas.

Beaucoup d'alcooliques boivent chez eux.
Ils ont le verre solitaire.

Avant cinquante ans : les plaisirs de la chair.
Après cinquante ans : les plaisirs de la chère.

Ce que Marie-Antoinette dirait des hommes d'aujourd'hui :
« Ils ont de la brioche ; qu'ils ne mangent plus de pain ! »

Dans certaines entreprises, il n'y a plus que les comptables qui
comptent.

Après plusieurs scandales boursiers, on se demande si le
système bancaire
ne devrait pas s'appeler système bancal.

Dans des réunions de chefs d'Etat, certains sont des potes
et d'autres des despotes.

Avec la hausse du prix du pétrole,
le transport aérien, c'est du vol.

Si le prix du pétrole continue à augmenter,
le sans-plomb va plomber votre budget.

Les pays occidentaux accueillent les dirigeants des pays
pétroliers en grande pompe.

L'abstention aux élections françaises expliquée par la pauvreté :
certains votent, d'autres vivotent.

Jadis les gens racontaient des blagues.
Aujourd'hui ils écrivent des blogs.

Le passé explique le présent,
mais il complique l'avenir.

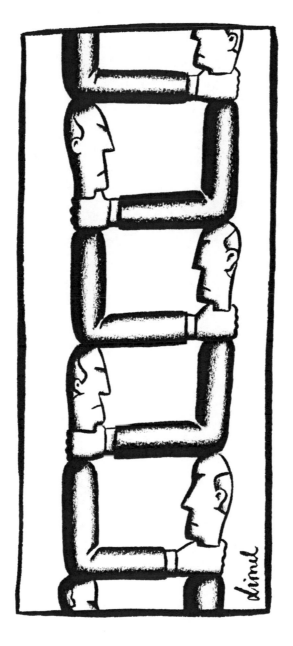

(Social Ladder)

Notes

[1] Jean-Marie Le Pen was the extreme-right contender for French President in 2002. His party has been declining since 2007.

[2] Oprah Winfrey is a popular American television star.

[3] In some English-speaking countries, signs say, "Bill Posters Will Be Prosecuted."

[4] PC means Personal Computer.

[5] PC also means Politically Correct.

[6] Y2K means Year-2000 compatible.

[7] A "small black" is a common name for *espresso* coffee in Australia.

[8] Hummus is a Lebanese dip made of olive oil and chick pea paste.

[9] The Australian federal capital is a small town inhabited mostly by civil servants and diplomats.

[10] Nicole Kidman is an Australian movie star.

[11] The Australian government deported Asian asylum-seekers to the Fiji Islands.

[12] Oxford Street is the center of the gay community in Sydney.

[13] The Queen of England is still formally the head of state of Australia.

[14] The *Tampa* was the name of a ship that rescued "boat people" seeking asylum in Australia in 2002.

[15] Pauline Hanson was the head of the nationalist political party "One Nation."

[16] Rupert Murdoch is an Australian-born global media mogul.

[17] Rabin square is the place where Israel's Prime Minister was assassinated in Tel Aviv, and named after him.

[18] The Palestinian Authority opened a casino in Jericho which operated from 1999 to the end of 2000.

[19] Temple Mount is the name given by Israelis to the Jerusalem hill on which the Jewish Temple was erected and later the Al-Aqsa Mosque built.

[20] Ehud Barak, Yitzhak Mordekhaï and Amnon Shahak, who were candidates in the 1999 election for Israel's Prime Minister, were former army generals.

[21] The Israeli government opposes a unilateral declaration of independence by the Palestinians.

[22] The Wye Plantation Agreement was negotiated in the U.S.A. between Benyamin Netanyahu and Yasser Arafat with the help of Bill Clinton in 1998.

[23] Ehud Barak was Prime Minister of Israel from 1999 to 2001.

[24] Hosni Mubarak is the President of Egypt since 1981.

[25] Jacques Chirac was the President of France from 1995 to 2007.

[26] Benyamin ("Bibi") Netanyahu was the Israeli Prime Minister from 1996 to 1999.

[27] United Nations Security Council Resolution 242 was adopted after the 1967 Six-Day War between Israel and Arab countries.

[28] United Nations Security Council Resolution 425 called in 1978 for the withdrawal of Lebanon by Israeli forces.

[29] Gen. Yitzhak Mordekhaï, Barak's Minister of Defense, was forced to resign over a sex scandal.

[30] Israeli soccer clubs are affiliated to a political party.

[31] The relations between Benjamin ("Bibi") Netanyahu and Bill Clinton were not always cordial.

[32] Under the Oslo accords, area "C" of the West Bank was under Israeli security control.

[33] Menahem Begin was Israel's Prime Minister from 1977 to 1983.

[34] Meretz was a left-wing political party which has been an ally of the Israeli Labor Party in government.

[35] Yossi Beilin was the Minister of Justice of Israeli Prime Minister Ehud Barak and an initiator of the Oslo Peace Process with the Palestinians.

[36] The Orient House was the unofficial headquarter of the Palestinian Authority in (occupied) East Jerusalem. It was eventually closed by Ariel Sharon in 2001.

[37] The Green Line is the name of the unofficial border between Israel and Palestine corresponding to the 1949 Armistice line crossed by the Israeli Army in June 1967.

[38] *Fatah* is the main political component of the Palestinian Authority.

[39] U.S. President Ronald Reagan called the Soviet Union the 'Evil Empire'.

[40] The CIS is the Commonwealth of Independent States, a loose alliance between some of the former Soviet Republics.

[41] "Trust but verify" was the motto of President Reagan in the area of disarmament.

[42] The German Democratic Republic is the former Communist East Germany.

[43] A 'have-not' is a non-nuclear weapon state.

[44] 'Friends of the Chair' are delegates appointed to mediate for solutions in a diplomatic conference.

[45] A 'killer-amendment' is an amendment to a draft resolution designed to void it from its content.

[46] Oxymorons are contradictions in kind.

[47] George Bush senior was the U.S. President when John Major was the U.K. Prime Minister.

[48] Bill Clinton was born in Little Rock, Arkansas.

[49] *Détente* was a French word meaning relaxation of tension, used during the Cold War.

[50] INF means Intermediate-Range Nuclear Forces.

[51] The 1968 Nonproliferation Treaty (NPT) by which non-nuclear weapon-states pledge not to acquire nuclear weapons and nuclear weapon-states, to disarm. India did manufacture nuclear weapons.

[52] From 1966 to 1995 France tested its nuclear weapons in French Polynesia in the South Pacific.

[53] In Latin, *Carpe diem* means: 'enjoy the day'. A "per diem" is a daily allowance.

[54] A non-paper is an unofficial, unattributable document introduced in a diplomatic negotiation.

[55] Voting on resolutions in the United Nations General Assembly is done electronically.

[56] For a long time the "Comprehensive Program of Disarmament" was on the agenda of the Conference on Disarmament.

[57] START means the Strategic Arms Reduction Talks between the U.S.A. and the Soviet Union, then Russia.

[58] Kool-Aid® is an American soft drink made from powder popular with children.

[59] M&M's® are small round colored, sugar-coated chocolate sweets.

[60] Band Aid® is a protective strip to cover small cuts and bruises.

[61] United Way is a large American charitable organization funded by donations.

[62] In the Mediterranean tradition, a man cheated by his wife is said to wear horns.

[63] In 2002, the U.S. Andersen law firm was convicted of obstruction of justice for shredding documents related to its audit of Enron, resulting in the Enron scandal.

[64] Tung Chee Wah was the Chief Executive of Hong Kong from 1997 to 2005.

[65] Actually a billion seconds ago (in 2006) it was 1974.

[66] If it is assumed that Jesus died in 33 AD, he would actually have been dead for 72 years a billion minutes ago (in 2006).

[67] DME: Distance Measuring Equipment.

[68] IFF: Identification "Friend or Foe."

[69] Of course, the International Institute of Answering Machine Answers does not exist. It was invented by the author of this compilation of "genuine" answers.

[70] Kings Cross is Sydney's "red light" district.

[71] The Lone Ranger was a popular television series that started in the late 1940s; its hero was a masked cowboy who always protected weak people from evil characters.

[72] WD-40® is an all-purpose lubricant in a spray can.

[73] Duct Tape® is a hard duty tape for use in odd jobs.

[74] Slinky® is a popular dog-like toy made of a long twisted spring funny to watch falling down stairs.

[75] Blockbuster® is an American home video rental company.

[76] ATM: Automatic Teller Machine.

[77] Styrofoam® is extruded polystyrene foam for construction isolation.

[78] Wal-Mart® is a popular supermarket chain in North America.

[79] All Bran® is a brand of cereal rich in fibers.

[80] Play Station®, Nintendo 64®, X-Box® are consoles for popular video games.

[81] Playing brandy means throwing a tennis ball hard at a player to make him or her lose points.

[82] A toy animated rabbit is the character of a famous series of TV commercial ads for Energizer® batteries.

[83] Clorox® is a popular brand for chlorine bleach.

[84] Lego® is a construction game made of plastic bricks.

[85] Play Dough® is soft colored dough to shape small structures.

[86] Super Glue® is a type of glue that bonds things very solidly.

[87] VCR means videocassette recorder.

[88] Shiraz is the Australian name for the syrah grape.

[89] Clingfilm® is an elastic transparent film used to wrap food for protection.

[90] SM: Sado-Masochistic (sextoys).

[91] Father Charles de Foucault was a French Catholic missionary in the early 20th century. Michel Foucault was a French philosopher and historian of the second half of the 20th century. Jean-Pierre Foucault is a contemporary popular presenter on French television.

Lightning Source UK Ltd.
Milton Keynes UK
21 April 2010

153118UK00001BA/2/P